DO YOU LOVE IT IN THE MORNINGS

?

The Progress Paradox

DO YOU LOVE IT IN THE MORNINGS

?

The Progress Paradox

Ronnie Apteker and Jeremy Ord

Media Africa and The Publishing Partnership

To Kiron, Leigh and all the other soulful people of this Earth ...

[
**The world is moving from
trading places to trading spaces.**
]

Published by Media Africa and The Publishing Partnership

First published in 1999

Copyright © Ronnie Apteker and Jeremy Ord 1999
The moral right of the authors has been asserted

ISBN 0 620 23904 2

Produced by The Publishing Partnership, 6 Pepper Street, Cape Town 8001

Edited by Arthur Goldstuck
Design by Cyn van Houten
Production Quality Control by John Morkel
Cover reproduction by Unifoto, Buitensingel Street, Cape Town
Printed and bound by Creda Communications, Eliot Avenue, Epping II

Acknowledgements

To Richard "Puppy" Came and Rob "Pumba" Taylor, whose sense of humour and zest for life have made a real difference to all of us. To our loved ones: Kiron and Leigh. To our children: Ashleigh, Michael and Kate. To our parents. And to Prancer. To all of you – thank you – for believing in us.

Special thanks to Charles Webster, Brandon Spear, Hillel Shrock, Rob Firer, Lara Little, Alon Apteker, Saki Missaikos, Becky Simmonds, Grant Ashfield, Kim Kramer, Derek Wilcocks, Andrea Maddocks and Michele Smith for all your input, guidance and valuable criticism on many parts of the text. And to Alison Wright, who will always be the first lady of cyberspace.

To Media Africa and The Publishing Partnership, the best publishing team we could have wished for. Arthur, you are 1 in 10001010101010101010101010010010101010101010100100.

Finally, to a few faceless people that we one day hope to meet: Stephen R. Covey, James C. Collins and Jerry I. Porras whose books, teachings and wisdom have been nothing less than inspirational. Much of what we have learnt these past few years has been guided by your ways of thinking. We are all experiencing new paradigm shifts, or simply put, new ways of looking at things, and this book contains a collection of those thoughts. Many ideas were borrowed from these great thinkers. Your "maps" have helped many of us find a better route.

[Contents]

[Ace]

PREFACE: A tale of two companies

I have worked at The Internet Solution (IS) for just over 5 years. This has been my first and only job. I have learnt about computers, about communications infrastructures, about online worlds and about people. The Information Technology (IT) industry is changing so fast that re-invention is a way of life.

You need to listen in the IT industry. To the trends, to the technologists, to your customers and to the people around you. We all spend so many years in school learning how to read, write and speak. But we never get taught how to listen. In the past five years I have learnt to become a better listener. The world is full of bad listeners, and I am one of them, but I am continually trying to improve. Progress has its problems and paradoxes – which is why I have put pen to paper and finger to keyboard.

Each technological advancement through the ages has had one objective – to save us time. Why then, do we seem to have none to spare? The Progress Paradox has never been more evident than since electronic mail made its grand entrance with the Internet's rapid growth. E-mail saves us so much time. It is the most efficient way to send documents, explore new ideas, share information, arrange appointments, communicate with your business partners, and more.

Why do we spend so much time behind our PCs wading

through e-mail for hours on end – and what do we get for it? And why do we panic when we are offline for more than 3 hours at a time? Seriously, with all this technological advancement we do not seem to have progressed – we have less time for real life than ever before.

Many people ask me why I work so hard. Probably the most fundamental thing I have learnt these past five years has to do with who works for whom: every time someone joins our organisation I have to work harder.

Empowerment is a word I have always known, but its true meaning I discovered only recently by looking within. I also learned that love is a verb. To love something you need to do something, continually and unconditionally. I love the company I represent, and I have to work harder every time a new person decides to join us and share our dreams and visions with us. I have to spend time empowering, guiding and listening to all the people that join us on our journey into the future. I met Jeremy "Jem" Ord on this journey.

In this book Jem and I share with you our developing knowledge about leadership, teamwork and professionalism, and we explore our purpose and values. We describe the new digital landscape that stretches further than the mouse can click. We highlight current trends and hint at the opportunities that lie ahead in the virtual world known as cyberspace.

This book is not intended to be a road-map to the information highway, but rather a collection of experiences and lessons that are helping us succeed in a world that moves forward at the speed of light. Computers are the easy part of life. It is the other stuff that is harder to work out.

We try never to forget that the work we do is for the people of our land. What does this mean? It means that in building the online world we try never to forget about end users. After all, it is their lives that we are trying to make easier.

Each technological step forward has been concerned with saving people time. That is what technology is about. We must never forget that IT is about saving time, working smarter and being more effective. *And we must always remember that with the wrong attitude it all means nothing.*

My brother taught many of us how to count ... two, three, four, five, six, seven, eight, nine, ten, jack, queen, king. Don't play cards with my brother. It was largely through his and Dave Frankel's leadership that we met Jeremy Ord and Dimension Data (Didata). IS and Didata are leaders in the IT arena. And as you may have guessed: we love IT. In the mornings, in the afternoons, and in the evenings. And we will love IT in the future. This is what we do.

We no longer count from ace to king, but we are constantly gambling with the future. The difference between this and real gambling is that we face a greater risk if we don't take this gamble than if we do. To get from jack to king, we must embrace the future, rather than treat it as a threat or a risk.

In 1996, my partners and I at IS decided to align ourselves with our new friends at Didata, as we all reset our dials and started pointing in the same direction: the virtual world and the future of online e-commerce. This book is partly about that journey. It is about win-win relationships, leadership, teamwork, professionalism, purpose, values and the Internet.

The only relationships that truly last forever are win-win relationships.

This is a time of globalisation. This is an era where spare time is rare. All the people we do business with are important. Their time is valuable. We continually strive to save our business partners time by minimising their exposure and maximising their returns. It is also about taking the risk out of the gamble we take with the future. We are confident that this book will help to do just that.

Ronnie Apteker
Founder of The Internet Solution

We first came across The Internet Solution (IS) some 5 years ago when Ronnie Apteker and Dave Frankel and a few other people had identified the Internet as being a particularly lucrative space in the years ahead, that and the fact that people would be using a different medium to communicate. At that stage there were two Internet companies in South Africa, IS and one other.

What we soon learnt about IS was that they were a bunch of very bright, dedicated "techno nerds" living on the Net, not going to bed. And many of them didn't have cars and they didn't really understand the true meaning of life. Life for them meant exploring the Web every night, meeting new people online and getting new digital things to play with. I am sure a lot of the time they were finding new jokes and new porn sites to look at, but that comes with the age and I think that as time passes one develops more of a business perspective.

My first recollection of IS was of this bunch of really bright guys with a vision for the future and a dedication to bringing the Internet to the man in the street; of making it more affordable and providing connectivity to all and sundry. In those early days we supplied them with equipment, sometimes on loan because they couldn't afford to pay for it, but always on the understanding that they would promote Dimension Data (Didata) and vice versa, which I think to a large extent did happen.

As time moved on and as we became more aware of the Internet and what it was going to do in our future lives, we forged a closer relationship with IS. That relationship evolved to a point where we felt we needed a strategic partnership or our own Internet company.

By that stage we had really come to know Dave Frankel, Alon Apteker and Ronnie very, very well, and we felt that we really couldn't do better in the South African industry, perhaps even globally, than by being involved with IS. They seemed to have the vision, they seemed to have the get up and go, and they seemed to have that good old Jewish "chutzpah" that makes things happen. And the people, while a lot younger than Didata (and Didata is a young company), had the same culture, the same vision and the same vibe. So ultimately we were able to convince IS that we should take a small stake in their company. That evolved to control of the company. Through all these periods, we have learned from one another about mutual respect, about trust, about the desire to make things work and, ultimately, that one has to share a common vision and a common strategy.

Once we took a stake in IS, it became the Didata strategy and vision that all Internet offerings would come through this vehicle. By not having total control of the company, the business was fragmented, with little initiatives starting up all over the place. This was recognised by both parties and, ultimately, a deal was concluded which has been mutually beneficial.

From a Didata Group point of view we have been nothing but impressed with the people, the culture and the drive in the company, to the extent that in 1998 we appointed both Dave Frankel and Alon Apteker to the board of Didata. They were then both about 28 years old. I think the appointment was a significant milestone. In the words of one of our strategic customers, a very respected person in the business world today, it was "visionary" that we put Dave and Alon on the board. They are the future of the company, and they are the guys who will be taking this company to new and greater heights as we proceed up our path in the global IT world.

I said that IS is about people, vision, hard work, and the desire to succeed. I must say all of those issues are evident in what we strive to achieve and in what we have strived to achieve in the past with Didata.

Within Didata I have been lucky enough to work with a lot of my close friends. Indeed, I would number among my closest friends in the world the people I work with. The fact that some of my old school friends and I still work together is of major significance. But more important is the way we operate and the way we try to employ people: through word of mouth, through culture, through friends. We almost have a hierarchy in some of our divisions where, if people are leaving or are going to get married or disappearing overseas, invariably they will introduce a friend to take over their position. This makes it very easy for us, because the friend knows what we are all about, and life continues for us without much loss in continuity.

In much the same vein as IS, I think Didata has been founded upon a basic common sense and an understanding that the IT environment is moving and changing every single day and that no two days are the same. Thus, we need to be aggressive, we need to be agile, we need to understand the market, and we need to make sure that we do not become complacent. Yes, we must not suffer from the "We have arrived" syndrome. This is the paradox of progress and of success.

I think we have been very lucky to create an inordinate amount of wealth for our people, but in order to attain that and in order to continue growing we have to be ahead of the pack, we have to be aligned, and we have to watch what the market is doing, both locally and internationally.

We need to be receptive to the market and, most important, we need to be aware of what our customers are saying. We need to listen. I think that, as with any company, it is important that we do not become arrogant, and that we remain close to our customers.

I think that what has always been apparent in Didata and throughout the group is that we are incredibly aggressive; it is important for us to be market driven and, when we go into a market, that we dominate that market. IS have a dominant market share in the areas of business they have chosen to be in, while Didata Networking and some of our other businesses are dominant market players in the markets they are in. This is not only in South Africa but also extends to 11 other countries, including Australia, the United Kingdom and several in Asia. The predominant theme is: if we are going to do it, let's do it well, let's be the market leader, and let's work very hard. At the end of the day, we say, let's enjoy each others' company.

Nothing gives me greater pleasure than when I get a phone call from one of my colleagues telling me about a successful day. For instance Ronnie phones me on a Sunday saying, "Jem, can I pop in for an hour to bounce an idea off you about a new venture?" That's great – and it says a lot about culture, it says a lot about the desire to work together and the desire to succeed. Our company culture is about sharing, empowering and listening. And our relationships are about friendship, support and winning. I always try to make time for the people I work with. After all, we are working together in a team and helping each other to make more of a difference in the world.

The Didata Group really has been blessed by having so many talented people, but people really cannot operate in isolation. They need to be supported by a team, so the teamwork aspect of this whole group has been of vital importance. As a reflection of our belief in teamwork, you will find a lot of people in our company who really enjoy sport. It is a major thrust throughout this group. In fact, the way that we project our corporate image is through sport.

We were an early sponsor of provincial cricket when isolation was still prevalent; we now sponsor a major golf tournament. Such sponsorship has become the major thrust of the group's corporate profile and, through that, we are able to develop very strong connections and retain very strong relationships with our key clients and partners.

I think a key strategy here is that we don't see relationships being built around myself or the senior people of IS, or any of the other group companies for that matter. We see the relationships extending right down the food chain and right up. It certainly extends to my assistant and to other secretarial assistants and admin staff: we believe that each one of them should be developing relationships with the people that we do business with. At the end of the day the people who fund our growth are our customers, and they are the people who pay our salaries, and they are the people who have allowed us to grow the group and to become very successful. Didata employs more than 8000 people around the world and will probably have a turnover of about $1.5-billion for 1999. It is our customers who have made this possible.

We always felt that IS should be the spearhead and the thrust of our Internet offerings in South Africa. And that has now extended to become a global vision. The team that runs IS is now responsible for taking our Internet initiatives and securing our Internet offerings around the globe to make sure that we are internationally competitive.

We live and work in an industry that does not and should not be accepting mediocre and average performance. Consequently, we don't allow group companies to grow at anything below market expectation. This means that, even though we are a $1.5-billion turnover company we expect to be growing at 50-60% per annum.

Many different paradigms and new ways of working will change business in the next few years. I think this is really where IT comes into its own. That is what this book is all about: challenging the current paradigms, challenging the way we do business today, and accepting – fortunately or unfortunately – that IT is here to stay.

IT is what it's all about – we had better start eating, sleeping and drinking Information Technology, because the world is going to revolve around information and technology. This is the progress paradox in a nutshell; that the information and the technology should be revolving around us, not the other way round.

Jeremy Ord
Chairman of the Dimension Data Group

Challenge the current paradigms, challenge the way you do business, and accept – fortunately or unfortunately – that IT is here to stay.

[Two]

What is a company?

Ask someone to think about the word "company". In fact, ask a group of people to take a piece of paper and write down what they think the word "company" means. We do this exercise with everyone who joins our organisation. Most people refer to a "business" or a "group of people making money" when defining the word "company". But the word really means "more than one person" or "a group of people". A marriage is a company. In fact it is called the institution of marriage, because it is such a special kind of company. A family is a company. A community is a company. So is a nation and a continent. We all collectively make up the company of people living on this planet. And yes, a business is another form of a company. We have many kinds of companies, yet the reasons that these companies are formed are the same across the board.

Making a difference is what a company is all about. People get together to form companies because they can do things together that they could not do on their own i.e. things that cannot be done by one person alone. It requires more than one to make a continuing difference in the world. And more than one means it requires company.

What are the fundamental reasons why people get together to form companies? This is another question we ask those who

It is better to
know some of the
questions than all of
the **answers.**

James Thurber

enter our domain.

We find that the vast majority of people will state that a commercial business' ultimate reason for being is to make money. We then ask people to compare a marriage, a business, a community and a country. Does a marriage exist to make money? Or a community? Or a country for that matter? Of course not. And if a company is simply a grouping of people then surely those people got together for reasons other than money? Why is a business any different from a marriage or a community?

Let us explore the reasons why individuals get together to form companies of people. When we do this exercise with new staff we generally get the following ideas being put forward:

- Working towards common goals and sharing common visions.
- Pooling of resources and exploiting diversity.
- Companionship.
- Balance and perspective.

Working towards common goals, two minds are better than one, and companionship. Lots of other descriptions arise too but they are generally restatements of these three ideas. Sharing common visions is very close to working towards common goals (and in a business one of those goals is generally to make a profit). In the case of a marriage, love is closely related to companionship. And pooling of resources is similar to two minds are better than one. We have only ever managed to describe four unique reasons why people get together to form marriages, businesses, communities, and other kinds of companies. The fourth reason most often does not surface in these discussions. But it is probably the most compelling - it is balance and perspective.

We have fun when we get together with other people. And we all know that other people have talents that may help us. If we communicate we will discover each others' goals and visions and perhaps share common ones. But balance is something that is often taken for granted. And perspective is something that is often passed over in a world where everyone talks so damn loudly and

We cannot do
great things
in this world,
only
small things
with **great love**.

Mother Theresa

aggressively, and nobody listens.

The ultimate reason for a company's existence should be obvious, but unfortunately it's not. When people say that a business' ultimate reason for existence is to make money then one needs to look seriously at Western values, and wonder what happened to the American dream. What is the ultimate reason for people getting married? What is the ultimate product of a marriage? And what is the point of this production? Yes, the word here is "produce". A marriage ultimately results in the production of offspring (if you don't agree then just stop and think how you got to be on this planet). And this next generation allows your legacy to continue. **Continuance is the ultimate reason for a company's existence.** All companies! Our organisation will continue long after we pass away. And our legacy will always be present as it guides newer generations into the years ahead. This is what two parents ultimately create when they enter into the company known as the institution of marriage.

A man and woman get together for love or companionship, for support or balance and perspective, to pool their resources, and to share visions and work towards common goals. Just think of the business you are involved in. How is it different to a marriage? These two kinds of companies are remarkably similar.

The ultimate reason for a company's formation is continuance. This country wants to continue to provide homes and opportunities for its future generations. And the community we live in wants to continue. And the business we work for wants to continue. Making money is simply one goal of our business. It is an important goal as the profits we make allow us to grow. Like your next meal, money is needed for growth. But it is not what makes us tick. Money is not the reason we work as hard as we do. **It is a mover, not a motivator.**

Let us look at some of the ideas that have been raised here.

Companionship is the easiest to absorb. People like being with other people. They enjoy each other's company. They have fun together and they share good and bad times.

Sharing common goals and visions is also easy to understand. People who have a thing for computers and technology, for

If you do not make a **difference,** you do not matter.

Tony Manning

example, generally get drawn to other such people. In the same way, people who want to study get drawn to a university full of students. They could study on their own, but they choose to go and be where other students are. They could play around on a computer at home, but most who love this field will typically join groups of other like-minded people.

This leaves us with the pooling of resources and balance and perspective. These are not so straight forward. Sure, "two minds are obviously better than one". But when has the pooling of anything been an easy task? And as for balance and perspective: we need to start listening if we are to exploit the advice of others. And how many good listeners do you know?

The pooling of resources means that we have to work through diversity. Two minds are better than one means we have to deal with difference. When has difference ever been an easy thing to get through? Just switch on CNN or pick up a history book. If something looks different we typically try to kill it. If something sounds diverse we try to stomp it out like a narc at a biker rally. So, why do people always respond so fast by saying that one of the reasons people get together to form groups of people is because they want to exploit their collective differences i.e. their synergies? Because in truth that is what we want to do. But in reality it is not that easy. Working through diversity is not simple.

People are different. Talent comes in all shapes and sizes. The pooling of people to synergise and create should result in a perfect world. But history tells us time and time again that working through difference generally results in failure. We are not referring to the failure of the custodians of this earth to live together and work together. We are referring to a business that goes bust. A primary reason why this occurs is because the members of that company could not work through their differences. No one appreciated the other's point of view. No one listened to anyone else. And no one gained any perspective from their colleagues.

Working through difference leads to creation. If you can take two minds and work through the differences that are brought about by such a union, then great things happen. Creation happens. It takes diversity to create. For a business to succeed it needs opportunities

Success *comes before*
*****work***** *only in*
the dictionary.

Vidal Sassoon

and ideas to be continually created. And this creation comes from the pooling of resources. Not an easy challenge. But definitely necessary for a company's continuance and well being.

Our organisation consists of sales people, engineers, marketing folk, accountants, human resource people, and so on. It takes all of these different kinds of people to create opportunities and growth. Working through difference is a big challenge to any growing company of people, be it a marriage, a business or a country. Often we are driven mad because those around us don't see our point of view. Because those around us are different. And we are wrong. It is not the differences in people that drive us crazy. It is the fact that we forget these differences. If Bill Gates calls his mother to rave about Microsoft's new Web site (still to be released) then Bill shouldn't go nuts if she does not seem to get excited. And why won't she be excited? Because like any mother, she wants grandchildren, and lots of them. And if Bill does go nuts then is it because his mother is different to him? No. It is because he forgot that his mother is different to him. What's on her mind is different to what's on his. If he goes nuts it is because he forgot that she was different. Don't forget: we are all different. And we have to respect these differences and work through them. Because if we succeed then great things can happen.

There is no creation without diversity. Only a man and woman can create a new life. Not a man and a man or a woman and a woman. It takes great difference to create something special. Men and women are very different and they have been driving each other mad as long as we can remember. But it is not the differences in men and women that drive each other crazy; it is forgetting these differences that results in full moon behaviour. In the same way here at our organisation we have sales people and engineers, for example. These are two very diverse groups of people. And they rarely agree on anything. But they are both necessary components in the creation of anything in our company. Pooling their collective talents in such a way as to create forward momentum, growth and profits is a big challenge.

Balance and perspective is also something you get by working through your differences. It is amazing how much you can grow

The reason worry
kills more people than
work **is that**
more people worry
than work.

Robert Frost

by listening to someone else's point of view. We have had so many ideas for new products and services that never got past the drawing board because someone pointed out a flaw in their overall plan for a particular initiative. Why do so many businesses fail? Is it because of bad products or lack of demand? Perhaps too many people in the company were doing their own thing. Perhaps no one appreciated anyone else. And perhaps no one had any respect for anyone else's talents or anyone else's point of view.

A successful business needs people to sell the product or service, people to create the product, people to collect the money, people to market the product, people to support the product, people to recruit more staff, people to direct the business, etc. Talk about diversity. Yes, it is a great challenge. But if you do it successfully then the creation of smiles will be worth the hard work. And not just smiles for today, but for the future. Future generations will hopefully learn from our efforts and from our mistakes. Our organisation will continue to thrive 100 years from now if the knowledge we discuss in this book is explored and understood.

We are all citizens of this world, custodians of the planet. We are all members of Earth. And our ultimate objective as a company of people is continuance. No one wants this planet to die. No mother wants her child to be brought into a world filled with radiation and terror. We all have one ultimate reason for being, and that is to look after the planet. (We are assuming here that life is defined in a physical sense, from the time you enter this Earth until the time you depart.)

The lessons we have learnt in our organisation are applicable to a marriage, a community and to this world. People get together to form a business because they can do something collectively that they could not do on their own. In the book *Built To Last* a very inspiring metaphor is used to illustrate this point: time telling vs clock building. One person can tell the time, perhaps for a lifetime. But many people can get together and build a clock that will tell the time long after they pass away. A clock can be viewed as the product of a group of people. A product that will endure for generations, perhaps forever.

In our organisation the products and services we provide are in the area known as Information Technology or IT. And yes, we love IT in the mornings. And in the afternoons, and in the evenings. And in the future. IT is what we eat, think, sleep and dream. We exist as a company of people to supply the world with more efficient ways of doing things by applying IT. We are ultimately concerned with making people more effective by saving them time by exploiting digital technologies.

IT is about working smarter. IT is about increasing productivity. Many people look to IT to boost their bottom line. The tools of the digital age can certainly play a role in this regard but companies should not look to IT solutions with this end in mind. The progress paradox is evident in this way of thinking. Instead of getting more out of life, companies adopt IT tools and spend less time living and more time earning i.e. they don't go forward in life, only in revenue. IT should be viewed rather as a means of enhancing a company's purpose. Invest in IT solutions so that you can free up time to focus on your core purpose.

If a company's reason for existing is simply to make money then it would make sense that they would look to IT to help boost profits. But if, for example, a company has the purpose of healing people with medicine, or making children smile, or applying technology to save people time, or whatever else, then it would be far more compelling to say that these companies would apply IT tools to allow them to concentrate on their core purpose. IT tools allow a company to reflect its reason for being, and to advance it. And this is where the idea of IT outsourcing was born. Outsourcing allows a company to focus on its core purpose.

A company's core purpose is about making a difference. IT is a tool that allows us to focus on this more clearly. IT also allows us to achieve more balance in life. IT frees up time so that we can make more of a difference and achieve more of a life balance. Well, that's the theory anyway. The progress paradox, however, tells us that this is not the case in practice.

It takes great difference to create something special. And if you succeed then the creation of smiles will be worth the hard work.

As if you could kill time without injuring eternity.

Henry David Thoreau

[Three]

Why, how and where

Every person on this planet has a talent. Everyone is an artist. Everyone has imagination and ideas. And everyone has a purpose. Think of a business as a picture. Initially, someone has the idea for the picture, then someone markets the picture, then someone sells the picture, and someone continually tries to create a bigger picture. A company is a collection of artists. And everyone has a role to play in the bigger picture. And yes, even the accountants or bean-counters are artists (we know – we have seen them in action many times). Managing, collecting and investing money collected from sales of the picture is an art form. Where do you think the term creative accounting came from?

A business is formed by a group of people who work together to provide some kind of service or deliver some sort of product. Every company will reach a point where its people start to think about and ask the big three questions:

- Why does the company exist?
- How does the company exist?
- Where is the company going?

Purpose implies why, values implies how, and goals implies where. Companies that enjoy enduring success have thought about

Quality is not an act, it is a habit.

Aristotle

these three simple words over and over. And much time has been invested empowering the members of these organisations with a better understanding of the answers to these three imperative questions.

Purpose

In the previous chapter we discussed why people get together to form groups of people or companies. In this chapter we explore the purpose of a company i.e. the results of a company's formation of which "making a difference" is key.

Most people assume that a business simply exists to make money. While this is an important result of any company it should not be the ultimate reason for the company's existence. People get together to build something collectively that will endure long after their time has passed. In the same way parents build a family and the ultimate purpose of a family is continuance. Parents create children who ultimately become parents themselves, and so the family continues and continues, keeping a legacy alive for hundreds, perhaps thousands, of years. Parents are the leaders of children. And if they succeed in their roles then they would have created further, future leaders in the children they produce. No parent wants to create children who are dependent. Independence is the desired state, and it takes guidance and leadership to create future leaders who are empowered to continue growing and making decisions. In the same way, a business needs to grow, produce future leaders, and continue. Money is simply an element, albeit an important one, that allows for growth. A family needs money to feed, educate and grow children. Money allows a company or a family to continue growing, but it is not their ultimate reason for being.

Purpose describes what a company actually does while it continues. It serves to guide and inspire the organisation as it journeys into the future. The key to purpose is not uniqueness, but rather authenticity. Many companies may have the same purpose yet may be radically different organisations – purpose does not necessarily differentiate. What makes one company more special than another is how deeply it believes its purpose in everything

Make little decisions
with your head.

Make **big** decisions
with your heart.

Author Unknown

that it does. Just think of a family: if the reasons that two people get married are not authentic then the purpose of that union will most probably be violated and a dysfunctional family will result. Just think about two people getting married where one member is in it for money – what kind of destiny awaits the offspring that may result from such a family? While this is a simple and expedient example of the fact that money should not be the reason that two people get married, it does illustrate the point quite clearly. In short, people form a company so that they can continue (their legacy in the case of a family, and their purpose in the case of a business). Money is one of the elements that allows for this to happen. In the case of a marriage the purpose is to continue with the family and its legacy. Often you will come across doctors who are the sons and daughters of other doctors, for example. Continuing a family legacy is evident all around us.

Purpose, in the case of a business, is to continue to provide some product or service. The authenticity of the mission differentiates one company from another. One family will always stand out above another if the reasons for those people coming together were based on deeper reasons beyond just the creation of monetary wealth. And so it goes for business and every other type of company. One business will always walk taller than its competitors if the people of that organisation are all in it for the right reasons. And purpose is what these reasons are about. Purpose, if it has been properly conceived, should be broad, fundamental and enduring.

Money gives us choice. And don't get us wrong, we love choice. Money allowed us, for example, to get this book published. We made the choice to put this book together because we had the resources to do it. The more money you have, the more choices you can make. But ultimately there is one choice that all of us think about, and that is whether to help others or not. Money allows you to do this. We wrote this book because we believe we have something to share with the world. We chose to help people by sharing our knowledge. **Money helps to give us this choice.**

He who has a "why"
to live for
can bear with almost
any "how".

Friedrich Nietzsche

Money and choice

Think about this: are you motivated by money? Most people would say yes. But when you think about it, money does not motivate anyone. Money moves people. Motivation comes from the fact that you enjoy doing something, that you feel fulfilled about the work you do. Motivation comes from inspiration, recognition and a sense of purpose. Many people do things they don't enjoy simply to earn money. A simple example will illustrate this point. Let's say we asked you to come and clean our toilets here at our offices (you should see them after one of our hectic chill out bashes, er, techno parties). And let's say we told you that you would love it, and you would feel good, and that you would get recognition beyond belief. Now think: do you really want to be the person who is recognised as the poor fool that was conned into cleaning the toilets? Is there anything we could say that would inspire you to help us? Would you feel fulfilled about doing this? No. But if we offered you a big pile of cash you would be there in a flash. Money moves people. But it does not motivate them. This of course does raise many obvious questions, as in: what motivates a janitor? The sad truth in this hard world we live in is that many people do things without any motivation. They do these things because they need the money to survive, and they do them without necessarily any chance for personal growth. With this train of thought in mind, we think that there must definitely be a close correlation between motivation and growth.

Different types of businesses will have different purposes. Businesses within the same industry sector may often have the same purpose (as in the case of two competing telephone companies, for example). What differentiates them is how they put their purpose into practice. A value system or a set of house rules describes how a company lives its purpose. Companies that have enjoyed enduring success have lived by a solid value system or code of conduct that is never compromised.

Purpose is something that is never reachable. A family can never stop continuing, and a business can never stop delivering its product or service. Purpose in the business sense may evolve over time as a company adapts to new markets and rolls out new

Let us be the *change*
we seek in the
world.

Mahatma Ghandi

services and product offerings. Values, on the other hand, never change. They describe how the company behaves, today, tomorrow and every day in the future.

Purpose describes what a business actually does today, tomorrow and every day into the future. Some simple examples will illustrate this. Disney exists to make children smile. Merck exists to help people through medicine. Sony exists to allow people to experience the pleasure and untold benefits that come from technological innovation. Boeing exists to improve the quality of life through technology and innovation. The company we represent exists to apply technology to save people time. Purpose guides us as we continue to use our imaginations, as we deliver products and services to the market. It gives us a set of parameters to work within so that we remain focused in our efforts. If someone within our organisation had to suggest that our company branch out into catering, say, just because we had many kitchens in our building, then we could simply take a look at our purpose and we would have to say no, as catering is not what we do. Purpose defines the space in which a company operates. Purpose may evolve over time and it often does inspire change.

Change is something that is always hard to work through, but absolutely necessary, especially in the IT industry. People constantly resist change, and continually talk of the "old days". This sentimental and romantic view of the "way things used to be" causes a lot of introspection instead of an outward view of the marketplace and external forces (competition, new trends, etc.) that are at work. Change can be seen as the end of something, or as the start of something new. Change brings about innovation, excitement and opportunities. Change may be one of the hardest things to deal with as a company grows. Change needs to be embraced, and it needs to be encouraged in today's competitive world. IT is one of those industries that constantly pushes the envelope to new boundaries as technology just evolves and evolves. Those stuck with old technology will die. Those who pioneer new ways of doing things remain at the cutting edge. People often have a love affair with a specific technology or methodology which can be really destructive. They tend to stick with something too long, and then they

Imagination is
more important than
knowledge.

Albert Einstein

abandon the entire company when they realise that they are work-ing in an old paradigm, instead of embracing change. Yes, chang-ing the way you think and operate, yet sticking firmly to a value system, while living a purpose, is an on-going challenge.

A company's purpose can never be achieved. Disney, for example, can never make children smile enough. There are always more children in the world, and tomorrow is always another day. In our organisation, we can never reach a point where we have applied all the technology that exists. We can never reach a point where we have saved people enough time. There is always new technology and people never have enough time. As long as we have imagination, as long as we remain artists, we will always find new ways to save people time by applying technology. Disney will always find new ways to make children smile. Boeing will always find new ways to enhance the quality of life. Merck will always find new ways to help people with medicine. And so it goes for all compa-nies. As long as we have creativity and energy, we will always find new ways to live our collective purposes.

Purpose may evolve over time. An organisation can never stop stimulating change and progress just by the very fact that pur-pose can never be completed. Our company, for example, existed originally to connect organisations to the Internet. Today, we con-tinue to live this mission, but we also build online Web worlds for our customers, we create electronic trading environments, we con-struct customer help-lines in the virtual world, and much more. Purpose should be simple, clear and extendible. Disney, for exam-ple, originally existed as a company that made cartoons. Today, the mission of making children smile incorporates cartoon making, but it has evolved far and beyond, to include theme parks, the Mickey Mouse Club, retail merchandising, and much more.

An important result of a well articulated purpose is that it defines a set of parameters in which a company operates. Disney, for example, exists to make children smile, and not to make people smile. Just think about what people smile at these days. Children should not be exposed to violence and sex when it comes to Disney's offerings – it does not form part of its mission. Whenever Disney delivers it has one intention: to make children

If you don't stand for something, you'll fall for anything.

Author Unknown

smile. And the more they make children smile, the more money they make.

At our company, we try to save people time by exploiting the wonders of IT. And the more effectively we do this, the more money we make. We will never attempt to sell someone technology if it's not going to ease a process, streamline a procedure, or do something that results in a more efficient activity. IT is about working smarter. It is about applying technology to become more efficient. That is our mission. That is why our company exists. And the more we are true to this mission (authenticity) the more money we make.

Everyone wants to make a difference in this world. Finding your purpose is what this is about. Making money is quite uninspiring if that is the principle reason for one's existence. But discovering a purpose or a reason and applying it can result in untold fortunes as one realises fulfilment, passion and the ability to make a meaningful contribution. At our company we work hard at making a difference, and the more we work at it, the more money we make. This is a simple realisation and a very powerful lesson in finding happiness. Make a difference. You too will make money as a consequence.

Values

A successful company continues to live its purpose by a set of values that are rock solid. These values make up the "how" part in the three questions. How defines the behaviour and attitude of a company's people. There is no universal accepted set of correct core values. You discover "how" by looking within. You cannot fake values. You either have them or you don't. Values are not open to change – they must stand the test of time.

A company typically will try to articulate about five things that it holds sacred. In our organisation we believe in professionalism, customer service, integrity, empowerment and fun as our core values. We strive always to be professional, both internally and externally. We endeavour to be customer focused, always acting with integrity. We attempt to empower our staff by listening and

Far and away
the best prize
that life offers
is the chance to work
hard at
work worth doing.

Theodore Roosevelt

by sharing. And we try to work hard and play hard. And we always stand firm in our beliefs, never compromising what we represent, and never violating our integrity. We are very passionate about our company and what it stands for. Our intense belief in our value system and our purpose is what drives this passion.

Our organisation is largely a people business. It is about people sharing ideas with people, it is about people proposing solutions to people, and it is about people working together. It is about relationships. We practise professional behaviour at all times, both internally with staff, and externally with customers. And we always strive for win-win relationships.

We have learnt who works for whom in our organisation. Whenever someone joins our company we have to work harder and listen more. We want all of the people who come on board to win. If they win, we win. It is that simple. And for them to win they need to be empowered. Their ideas need to be heard. And they need to make a difference. Our jobs are to make sure that they can make a huge difference.

Products and services evolve over time, leaders pass away, markets change, new technologies emerge, and strategies come and go, but our values remain the same. A company's value system is the glue that binds all the people together. And there is no set of right or wrong values. You discover values by introspection. A company should never change its value system in response to market changes but, rather, it should change markets if necessary. It must always remain true to its core values.

Again, your values should be authentic; you can put this to the test by asking: if you got out of bed tomorrow and were financially independent, would you continue to hold those values as sacred as the day before? Can you see those values being as valid for you well into the future as they are today?

Think about the stakeholders in your organisation. There are many more than just the shareholders. Every customer. Each supplier. The staff. The families of the staff. The government (a company pays tax). And even the community. When we build an online service like electronic banking, for example, every member of the community who uses that service saves time. Each person who is

Win-win is a belief in a third alternative. It's not your way or my way; it's a better way, a higher way.

Stephen Covey

helped by our efforts is a stakeholder. And the more they win, the more we win. If we save the community time with our efforts, then our services are going to become more popular and the demand for our work will increase. And then we win. And provided we never stop thinking of the end user, the customer, we will always come up with new ways to save them time by using our imaginations in the application of Information Technology. In our relationships (between IT company and end user) there needs to be mutual benefit. All our stakeholders need to win.

Making money or maximising shareholder wealth is always the grey, uninspiring, off-the-shelf mission statement that will be heard in those circles where a core purpose has not been identified. We could make money in our organisation by selling people technology they don't really need. But this would violate our purpose and it certainly would contradict our value system. It would not be in the best interests of our stakeholders. The end users would not win in this case, and ultimately, neither would we. Trust is the fundamental building block in life, and it is needed to build any win-win relationship. The more we continue to deliver time-saving technologies, the more people will trust us to continue doing so well into the future. The more we make a positive difference to people's lives, the more all of our stakeholders will win. That is what win-win is all about.

Our company's values may only be meaningful to the people within our organisation, and there is nothing right or wrong about that. If someone does not agree with our code of conduct then they may decide not to join our organisation. You cannot force values onto people. Values are something you feel and hold sacred. You find them inside of you. If you don't believe that customer service is a value, for example, then you may choose to work in an organisation where customers are not part of the day to day profile. Sony, for example, does not view customers as central to its core value system. And this makes sense when you think about it: when was the last time you bought something from Sony directly? You didn't. You buy products from consumer goods stores. Sony does not deal with you directly. And perhaps that way of thinking is what you believe. Either way, there is no right or wrong here. It is what

There is a close connection between **getting up** in the world and **getting up** in the morning.

Author Unknown

you genuinely believe deep down that is fundamental.

The people within a company need to commit to the organisation over the long term and a well defined value system can help in defining who is in and who is out. A clearly articulated value system attracts to an organisation people who buy into the company's ways of thinking, and conversely, it will repel those people who do not agree. You cannot make people believe in something. They either do or they don't. And if they choose to leave because they find that they are incompatible with the company's core ideology, then welcome that outcome.

You never want anyone to undermine what you stand for and you always want to retain your value system. So, if people within a company do not fit in, then let nature run its course. People who share the same value system and purpose often do not necessarily all look or think the same. Artists and talent come in all shapes and sizes. A company is a world filled with diversity and with different viewpoints and ideas. The key is that they all believe in the same value system, and that they all share the same purpose.

In our company people are encouraged to come up with new ideas. We encourage our people to think differently. If someone has an idea which we think is exciting we say, "Go and develop a business plan." And if we think it is viable we will then say to that particular individual, "Are you going to run it? Tell us how you are going to do it. What budget do you need? Go and make it work." And that is an incredibly powerful motivator for our staff as they can dream up new initiatives and know that they are not going to be shot down. They are encouraged to get on with it. And that is what IT is all about – IT is about change. It is about constantly challenging the norm.

Goals

Goals are what give a company forward momentum. The "where" is the third question that continually changes as goals are met and new ones set. Goals have consequences, positive if achieved, and negative if not. Accountability is a key aspect in the setting of goals. The individuals in an organisation have to understand the up and

Making money is <u>art</u> and
working is <u>art</u> and
good business
the best <u>art</u>
of all.

Andy Warhol

down sides of a particular goal. We set many, many goals in our organisation. From the growth in the numbers of staff, to their training, to customer growth or market share, to awards that we are keen to win and, of course, to profit targets that we set. Money is the easiest to understand. If we reach certain targets that have been set from a financial point of view, then we have more wealth we can distribute, invest and utilise. If we don't, then the negative consequence is that there is less money for training, equipment, leisure, salaries, and so on. In short, we make money and we use it for growth. If we don't make money we don't grow.

How many times in the past have you heard someone refer to "the art of making money"? Yes, it is an art. It takes different types of artists working together to create ideas, excitement, opportunities, growth and wealth. All of these artists need to be aligned with the company's values and purpose. All of them will have different goals that need to be met. A profit target is just one of them.

Our company focuses largely on that area of IT known as computer networking. To network is to live. We all start networking the day we first enter this world. **The opposite of networking is not-working.** But networking in today's world brings about an interesting paradox. We work with more and more people but we have less substantial and less trusting relationships. Thanks to constantly renewed technologies we have the ability to communicate with more and more people, each day, from a global perspective.

But are we really progressing?

Medical technology, for example, has added years to life. But have we added life to years? Information technology allows us to communicate more, at lightning speeds, on a global basis, with people we most often never get to meet face-to-face. Is this really progress?

People often appear to be very insecure about themselves these days. Perhaps technology has contributed to the progress paradox. Perhaps there is a limit to the number of meaningful relationships a human being can experience in a lifetime. Perhaps technology is forcing us to have too many superficial relationships instead of a few meaningful ones that are based on real trust.

Perhaps trust is being replaced by numerous superficial interactions. Perhaps the building blocks of relationships are being undermined by technological innovations.

We think that the diminishment of trusting relationships in the world is related to how wired everyone is becoming. And this trust deficiency is creating insecurity.

Yes, we are trading quality for quantity. Many of life's bigger questions have their answers buried right in this very point. A balance most definitely needs to be struck. In the third question pertaining to where, let balance be one of the most important goals that we all address.

Discovering your purpose and applying it can result in untold fortunes as one realises fulfilment, passion and the ability to make a meaningful contribution to the world.

[Four]

We both have a view, ok?

Read the text below. Once you have read it, go back and count the number of times the letter "F" appears.

> FINISHED FILES ARE THE RESULT OF YEARS OF
> SCIENTIFIC STUDY COMBINED
> WITH THE EXPERIENCE OF YEARS.

How many "F"s did you see? The most common answer is 3. This is an old and popular psychology exercise that illustrates a very good point: we all have a different view. We do this exercise with all the people who join our organisation and most of them see 3 "F"s, but some see 4, and some see 5, and some see 6. And people with a lot of imagination even see more. Each "E" could be an "F" with a little inspiration. All you need is a new way of thinking, a new way of seeing things, a new perspective, and you will be amazed how much further the eye can see. In the computer world the common buzz-word phrase is "paradigm shift". A new paradigm represents a new way of seeing things.

The correct number is in fact 6 "F"s. Each of the "of"s contribute to this phenomenon because often we tend not to see that which is familiar. Even people with incredible attention to detail miss the "of"s. Only people who cannot read and write always see

Those who **learn** the least generally **talk** the most.

Alon Apteker

6 "F"s without fail. But who is right? Everyone. There are 3 "F"s. But there are also 4 or 5 or 6. Yes, everyone has a different view on this, and everyone's view is valid. Like the title of this book, it is seen differently by different people.

In the same way, everyone has a different view of the Internet. Some see it as a collaboration and research tool, others see it as a new retail channel, while yet others see it as an IT support tool, and yet another bunch will see it as a collection of wires and computing machines. And all of these views are right. The Internet is all of these things and more. We all see things differently. Appreciating this difference is a huge challenge.

Everyone on this planet has a view on every single thing. Whether you agree with a specific view or not, is not as important as whether you affirm what someone else has to say. Listen to other people - you will be amazed at what you can learn.

When it comes to relationships, listening is very important. Fundamental, in fact. Appreciating someone else's point of view and accepting their differences is a key factor in establishing win-win relationships. "Two minds are better than one" is easy to say but not so easy to put into practice. In relationships we often tend to take things for granted, especially the common things. We often take it for granted that people are, in fact, listening. Well, the world is full of bad listeners, and in our company we are continually trying to improve this.

We spend over ten years in school learning to read, write and talk, but not to listen. God has given us two ears and one mouth, and there is a reason for that ratio – we all talk too much; we need to listen more.

Listening is an art. Just think about how many ways there are to listen. How often have you been on the telephone while reading your e-mail in the background? Are you really listening? How often are you just dying to have the last say when someone else is speaking? Empathic listening needs to be mastered and appreciated.

We have learnt that the easiest way to piss someone off in this world is: just to ignore them. Remember, you learn nothing by speaking. If you want to be in control you need to listen.

You **teach** best
what you most
need to **learn**.

Richard Bach

Everyone on this planet is a sales person. Selling requires you to listen. Everyone is trying to close some deal, convince someone of something, negotiate some terms or get something done. How many times have you tried to sell to your parents? Yes, we all do it. Selling is an art. If you really want to be good at it, you need to listen. The old school thinking of shouting as loud as you can has long been disproved as an effective mechanism for producing results. If you really want to form meaningful partnerships with your staff and your customers you need to listen to each other. You need to appreciate each other's points of view, and you need to work together. Listening is a key to working together in a successful manner. Work together – "we" compete better than "I". We have enough competition in the market-place, we don't need to bring it into our organisation. In our company we continually strive to become better listeners. We always try to pool our views and come up with a better one, together.

Leadership is about listening. Parents need to listen to their children to understand them, to guide them, and to encourage them. Parents have more perspective and more wisdom than their children, and their job is to use their knowledge to teach their children, who will one day most likely be parents too, a better way. And this is accomplished much more effectively when one understands the challenges that children represent. In the same way, new people who continually join our company are looking for guidance, knowledge, growth and happiness. Our jobs are to teach them and to create future leaders. And listening is fundamental in this continuing process.

Team work requires people to listen to one another. It requires working through diversity. It requires the pooling of ideas. It requires an appreciation for different viewpoints and opinions. Like a family, a team needs leadership, and the ultimate function of these leaders is to produce more future leaders. Parents have the ultimate job of raising children who will one day themselves become parents in the future. And so it goes, on and on. Continuance requires the creation of more and more leaders.

What do leaders have that make them stand out? How did they get to have these attributes? And when it comes to business,

The function of **leadership** is to produce more **leaders,** not more followers.

Ralph Nader

what has to happen for new leaders to emerge? A leader generally has more perspective and wisdom than other people in the organisation.

We have a very flat organisational structure in our company. **The only hierarchy that really exists is one that is characterised by knowledge.** The people at the top of the company have more perspective and insight as to where the company is going, and as to why the company does what it does.

If you want to grow in an organisation you need to learn as much as you can as to why the company exists, how it exists, and where it is going. The best way to learn is to listen. Listen and learn. And lead.

Effective leaders are generally better listeners than most.

Leaders typically get replaced when they start to demonstrate a warped sense of perspective and when they start to neglect the stakeholders in the organisation. Leaders serve those that they lead. **When a person joins our company we always have to work more, not less.** We have learnt who works for whom in our company. Every time someone comes to work in our organisation we need to invest time to empower them, guide them and listen to them. This time is precious. Time is so valuable. We spend this time with new staff because we see it as an investment rather than an expense.

Leaders in an organisation serve those people that they employ. Leaders therefore have to work harder as a company grows and grows. Leaders work for the people they serve, for the people of their organisation. This means that as the company grows they actually have more responsibilities, and have to work more, not less.

We want all the people who join our company to realise as much of their true potential as possible. We want them to win. We want them to grow. We want them to become future leaders. That is the only way we can continue to live our purpose. The continuance of our company and what it stands for requires all of our stakeholders to win. It requires us to empower our staff as much as time allows, so that future leaders can emerge.

We have heard of so many people saying how they want to grow in our organisation and how they want to eventually become

*It is **not fair** to ask of others what you are **not** willing to do **yourself**.*

Eleanor Roosevelt

managers. Everyone wants to manage people. Well, we have learnt that you should never want to manage people. You manage things. And you lead people. You manage a sale, the inventory, the money, but you lead people. You listen, and you teach and empower them. You show them the way. Just like parents who show their children what's right and wrong, and how to be better than they were.

Everyone on this planet has imagination. So, let them use it. Combine their ideas, work through diversity, and create. It takes difference to create something meaningful. Respecting and appreciating someone else's point of view requires humility and an open mind. Don't be proud. Show people you care, and be honest about it. In our company professionalism is a key value. So is empowerment. We strive to keep a cool head at all times. We try and listen to one another with enthusiasm and mutual respect.

Empowerment means showing people the way. It means teaching them how and allowing them to ask questions. By simply telling people what to do without any chance to explore why is very dis-empowering. By not listening you dis-empower someone completely. Trust is the fundamental building block in any relationship. Trust is built by empowering one another. By respecting one another. By appreciating difference. By exploiting diversity to everyone's benefit.

Are you humble? Do you trust the people you work with? Do you see that others may have some knowledge that you don't? Do you realise that you always have so much to learn? Do you realise that this is one of the reasons that makes life so exciting? Learning is what life is about. Every day we wake up, and every day it is our God-given right to realise more of our true potential. As leaders we continually try to produce future leaders. That means we need to build trusting relationships. And we need to listen to what others can teach us.

As a company that provides IT solutions we need to understand our customers' points of view. That means we need to listen to them. We need to appreciate their ideas, and we need to demonstrate our IT knowledge, so that together, we can come up with a mutually beneficial solution. A healthy partnership means that both parties are better off working together. Win-win relationships are what we are continually trying to build. Respecting another point of view is fundamental in this regard.

When working through difference it is important to try to keep things simple. Don't be pretentious. Be humble and be open. It is much easier to affirm what people say if it is easy to understand. Don't complicate things. **Remember: KISS – Keep It Short and Simple.** And pay attention. It is a lot harder to drive someone crazy with attention than you think. You can never care too much, you can only care too little.

Technology allows us to communicate in so many different ways. Yet, with all these fantastic tools we don't seem to be learning as much as we should. We have new ways of speaking, but not of listening. People talk of information overload quite often these days. Perhaps there is just too much noise pollution in the world, and perhaps what we need is some silence, some time to listen. Switch off that cell-phone when you are sitting down to discuss something with someone. Don't fiddle with your laptop and read your e-mail when you are in a meeting. Pay attention, and listen.

Nothing is worse than having to interrupt someone in the middle of some important discussion with an intrusive, high-pitched, screeching cell-phone. Yes, we have gone forward technically, but are learning less. Technology allows us to make more noise than ever before, to say so much, but it is not helping us to listen.

We all see things differently. Appreciating this difference is a huge challenge. Appreciating someone else's point of view and accepting their differences is a key factor in establishing win-win relationships.

[Five]

Chicken or the egg?

Computers are about storing and retrieving data that is represented digitally by an array of 0s and 1s. Music, video, text, photographs, catalogues, you name it, can all be digitised, stored and manipulated on a computer. The Internet is a digital transport mechanism that forms the highways that join up the computer networks of this world. So much information exists on digital media, but more often than not it has been so far away. The Internet has made the world much, much smaller. Everything is becoming a mouse click away.

So, which came first: the skyscraper or the telephone? Where did the word "hello" come from? And have you ever heard such strange questions before in your life? Well, we have the answers, so read on. The telephone came first. The word "hello" came about after the telephone. Think about it ... who would want to, or more insightfully, who could work on the 50th floor of a sky-scraping office tower without a telephone? How would you get anything done? How would you communicate? How would you get business? How would you process orders? How would you survive?

Without the telephone everyone would need their own private elevator, and everyone would be going up and down all day long, in and out of buildings, physically going from one customer to the next. Then there are your suppliers, auditors, advertisers, and many others. How would you talk to them all? Face-to-face? There wouldn't be enough time in the day to make the money to pay the landlord.

The telephone liberates. It allows us to live vertically. Without the telephone and the PABX (telephone switchboard), a corporation would want (and need) ground level offices because all their business activities would be done on the street. It would be like a giant flea-market. And this makes sense if you think about it. Flea-market stalls don't have telephones and PABXs. If they did they would be sitting in high-rise buildings and not in a flea-market. Have you ever heard of a flea-market stall with a half a million Rand PABX? The argument works from any direction. And the direction here is up – the telephone allows for vertical living and working. And the Internet takes this one step beyond.

The Internet, and more specifically the World Wide Web, allows a company to profile itself online, provide value-added customer services, publish product and service information, and much, much more. Value-added services can be created and exploited via the Web in ways that were not viable in the physical world. Media companies like Times Media Limited (TML), for example, can provide cost-effective search facilities of past publications online which are simply not feasible in the physical world. Imagine the resources that would be needed if you called up TML and asked them to copy every article that dealt with the Internet over the past 3 years and fax these to you. Computers have always been good at storing and retrieving data. The Internet provides us with the infrastructure that is required to exploit this phenomenon at a distance. And the Web gives us a multimedia platform to extend a corporation's tentacles into the alleyways of cyberspace.

In coming years we are going to see SET-compliant online merchants. The Secure Electronic Transaction protocol, developed jointly by VISA and MasterCard, is going to change everything. Let's review: In 1993 we saw the first Internet Service Providers (ISPs) setting up world-wide. Quick off the mark in South Africa, we saw IS (The Internet Solution) establish itself in that same year as this country's first commercial ISP. A host of non-profit and academic operations were also introduced in that year. Simultaneously we saw the emergence of the hyper-text transfer protocol (http), better known in its use as the Web, and a crude public domain browser called Mosaic made its entrance.

Towards the end of 1994, we also witnessed the first version of the browser-deluxe from Netscape (actually Netscape was originally called Mosaic Communications but changed its name because of confusion around the original Mosaic browser). In 1995 Netscape's Navigator became the *de facto* browser of choice and the world's corporations started to view the Web as the new place, er space, to set up shop. Not much happened in terms of electronic commerce that year, but the foundations were clearly evident. In 1996 we witnessed Microsoft's infamous agility as they embarked on an aggressive Internet strategy. Again, the world's corporations embraced the Web that year and started high-tech, high-octane online marketing initiatives. In 1997 Microsoft's IE (Internet Explorer) became the other mainstream Web browser and Netscape's dominance would be lost forever. Microsoft's policy of giving IE away for free was a sure thing. Try and compete with that on price!

In 1997 we saw electronic banking make its debut as four South African retail banks all launched online financial services. And in the years immediately to come we will see the merchants of this land trading online. SET-enabled Web sites will be the order of the day, and the gold rush to vend online will be in full flight before you know it. And the "browser", in the near future, will be a thing of the past as the "shopper" becomes the new norm. After all, we were all born to shop, not to browse – online or off.

So, what came first? The telephone and then the skyscraper. Then came advanced communication systems followed by the emergence of the world's giant corporations, which exploited the opportunities presented by various information technologies, allowing them to create world-wide distribution networks and powerful global brands.

And then came the Internet and the Web, followed by secure transaction processing ... and presto, a whole new world was born. And this new online, virtual world will transform our lives at warp speed. We are pretty sure that Christmas shopping this year will involve a lot of mouse clicks!

Digital real-time estate

Digital communication is what the Internet is all about and the digital world is like any other world. It has good parts and bad parts. Prime real estate in the online world is the place, er, the space to be. Any company launching an online, interactive service on the Web should consider where they are going to house their future marketing machines and money spinners. In the physical world of bricks and cement the modern-day mall represents hot property. These places are where all the shoppers are. The shoppers represent traffic. And traffic means business.

Why don't you go shopping in another country? Because it is too far to drive. Simple. People want service. And they want it now. So they go to a place that is full of shops, full of goods and services, and full of attentive traders. The modern day mall represents real-time physical service. Real-time online service is no different. It is in demand. The difference between a few seconds and tens of seconds in the online world is like the difference between driving (and parking for that matter) for 20 minutes as opposed to many hours. No one drives many hours to go shopping. The same goes for the virtual world. People on the Net want fast, responsive online Web services. These digital shops need to be housed on prime real estate to provide for supremo quality of service parameters.

There are many components that encompass hot property. In the physical world, the modern mall is prime real estate. This phenomenon is constituted by colourful shop windows, accessibility, floor space, access roads and parking. The same goes for the online world. Hot Web space is characterised by a combination of virtual shop windows or HTML (HyperText Markup Language) pages, accessibility (the faster the response time of the Web offering, the better), disk space (the more disk space you have the more you can sell), network infrastructure (the digital roads that connect the users on the Net to the Web), and parking (the greater the number of visitors or "hits" the Web server that houses these HTML pages can handle, the better).

Many people often want to see a sample or a snapshot of the virtual world. As you can understand, it is not that simple. The digital world and the physical world are very similar. To casually say that the virtual world is all about computers is only correct at a micro level. When someone asks for a sample of a physical building you cannot present that person with a brick. Bricks, like computers, are the building blocks. Put your bricks in the wrong area and no one will want to rent them from you. Your bricks need to be accessible, well maintained and, basically, hot. The same goes for computers. Virtual malls need to be accessible, responsive and hot. Hot is the key word here. By hot, we mean attractive, exciting and bursting with imagination. And the points described above are the mainstream ingredients in the creation of a sizzling cyberspace.

We heard a very insightful comment a few months ago that explained the importance of utilising decent real estate in the digital domain. When your company launches an online world on the Web, do so with the right electronic infrastructure. You may have a great company, with exciting products, and business may be booming. If so, the chances are you probably have colour brochures and glossy pamphlets as well. And we are sure you don't produce these company documents on scruffy paper with ink that smears. So, when you are considering publishing information on the Web, and ultimately vending online, use the same quality materials in the virtual world. Solid ink on quality paper means good graphics (aesthetically pleasing images, intuitive icons and quick download times are what define good graphics on the Web) on a fast Web server. A fast Web server means decent network infrastructure, robust and reliable hardware, and quick response times. Check on these parameters when you go house hunting for cyber space.

When you think about the virtual world take a step back and get physical. Get your mind into physical mode. Everything that applies to the concrete world has a direct counterpart in the virtual world of cyberspace. Use the right tools for the job, be it physical or virtual, analog or digital, or whatever. Virtual tools do exist. They may be harder to touch but they are there.

Digital difference

Doing things digitally represents a major paradigm shift. To make sure you avoid the progress paradox when steering virtually, always remember that if the goods are worthwhile, they will sell offline and online. We have seen many people invest in IT only to go backwards in terms of their retailing effectiveness. Remember, doing it digitally means adding value, saving time, making it more accessible, and making it easy to use. Keep these parameters in mind.

The Internet is an infrastructure – not a product or an information service – and it competes with other infrastructures.

The Internet is not in competition with Reuters, Dow Jones or AOL (America Online).

What the road-system is to motor cars, the Internet is to computers. The phrase "time is money" is nowhere better understood than on the Internet. As an alternative to traditional communications infrastructures, it has no equal. The time spent delivering and receiving messages, information and products, is minimised by the electronic nature of computer networks. There are, of course, other proprietary infrastructures in existence, but they are not mainstream. A mainstream communications infrastructure is characterised by a network that is accessible to the general public: roads, postal system, telephone network, fax and the Internet. Each infrastructure competes with the others in terms of efficiency and appropriateness (you would generally not order a pizza using the postal service, although it is possible).

Ask the next person you speak to for their business card. The chances are there will be at least four contact addresses on the card (in addition to their name of course). These addresses represent communications infrastructures – four mainstream ways of communicating with that person. The most obvious of these is the physical address (this is most probably how you got the card in the first place). Physical infrastructure is used when a meeting is required – a face-to-face, live, physical, meeting. The other three infrastructure addresses that are typically on the card would include: postal address, telephone number, and fax number. Some people print their cellular numbers on their business cards, and nowadays, Internet e-mail and Web addresses too.

Private infrastructures also exist and are generally more expensive to use. These are value added networks (VANs) and are used when urgency, privacy, and reliability are of primary concern. Communicating using private infrastructures is more costly but generally more efficient and reliable. Each country has its own such proprietary networks or infrastructures.

A VAN is a privately operated communications network. In the Internet world, a VAN is made up of wires and computing machines. A VAN is characterised by secure and predictable communication channels between different parties on a public infrastructure. By secure we mean that data in transit remains private and by predictable we refer to the time taken to send and receive the data. VANs are created by exploiting public networks in such a way that simulates private communications channels between two or more parties. A private communications mechanism by default is secure and predictable, as opposed to a public network that is open to abuse and is often congested.

Creating a VAN via the Internet allows for the safe passage of data with committed information rates (response times) in a highly cost-effective manner. A VAN is a generic concept. A computer network is only one kind of VAN. Service companies utilising non-computer-based infrastructures may establish VANs on top of these networks.

Courier firms represent one type of a VAN, for example, with international offerings in the form of Federal Express, UPS, and DHL. Each of these proprietary infrastructures still use the same roads and airways as the mainstream infrastructures, but they compete with the mainstream infrastructures by adding value to the underlying service. The underlying service is communications – getting your message from A to B. If the message is important and private, and needs to be timeously delivered, people will pay a premium for this convenience.

Digital driving

When one takes to the roads there are certain procedures that must be followed. Firstly, you should own or have access to a motor vehicle. Next, you need to learn how to drive. In fact, we could say that you need to get "automobile literate". This does not mean that you have to understand the internal workings of the combustion engine, but you should know that the vehicle needs to be filled up with petrol, the air pressure in the tyres needs to be correct and, of course, you need to know how to operate the vehicle. Finally, you need to learn some protocols, or rules of the road: drive on a specific side of the road, stop at red traffic lights, and don't drink and drive.

The same goes for the postal service, the telephone system, the fax network, and so on.

When you use the telephone you need to understand some basic protocols of communications over this voice-orientated network. "Hello", generally is a good starting point. You need to learn how to drive a telephone, er, dial a number.

Each infrastructure has protocols, and machinery. Some of them are very simplistic and finite, others are difficult to comprehend. The Internet is the latest mainstream infrastructure and is the most difficult to absorb. The fact that you need to be able to "operate" a computer is probably the most overwhelming aspect about getting online. Except that you don't need to be a computer programmer or a rocket scientist to do this. You simply need to know how to point and click.

The machines used on the Internet are computers. Computers of all denominations. Computers are not easy things to understand. We see so many people flocking to evening computer classes so they can become computer literate. There seems to be a fear that if you do not "learn" computers you will be left behind. This is like saying: "I need to learn cars". You learn how to drive so you can get around, but you don't need to learn about the cold metallic monster beneath the bonnet. So when people say they need to be computer literate, what they really mean is they need to learn how to "drive" a few popular applications, like a word processor or spreadsheet. And, these days, a Web browser.

Before you go surfing the Internet, learn to swim in the ocean, or at least understand the basic attributes of the personal computer so that you don't ask questions like: "my mouse has frozen, did *www.playboy.com* cause that?" This is like saying: "I ran out of petrol, is it Pizza Hut's fault?" You only need to understand the fundamentals of computers. What makes a computer application tick? Or talk, for that matter?

A computer consists of hardware, firmware and software. There are many alternative ways to put these components together, but each computer is generically the same. The hardware is the actual physical machine (the PC), the firmware is the operating system, and the software comprises those applications that run on the operating system. These days most people who use PCs typically go for a Pentium with Windows 98 and the Microsoft Office suite of programs that include a word processor (MS Word) and spreadsheet package (MS Excel). Hardware is the solid stuff. Software is the not so solid stuff. It is, well, er, soft. Firmware is also software but without the solid stuff it's useless. That is why it is called firmware – it needs to have a firm presence or else the soft stuff has nowhere to run. The firmware is what gives the PC its personality. Although it gets upgraded every few years its fundamentals remain the same. Understand a computer and you will save yourself sleepless nights, and you will also learn to ask more insightful questions if you get lost on the information superhighway.

If you have driven a Volkswagen all your life and then you strike it big (perhaps you started an ISP in the early days) and you go on to buy a Mercedes, you don't have to learn how to drive all over again. Generically, every car is similar to every other car. They all have an engine (hardware), an operating system consisting of pedals, gear sticks, etc. (firmware), and perhaps even some applications that allow you to calculate fuel consumption and average cruising speed (software).

Digital detours

The very first infrastructure to become mainstream was the physical infrastructure. We take it for granted, but the naming of roads and the assigning of street numbers was a major advancement in networking. It is the first modern evidence of domain naming and intelligent routing. Imagine being told to go left at the old tree and then carry on until you reach the rock and then 100 paces in front of you, can't miss it – it's much easier to say 101 First Street.

Physical infrastructure is the most pervasive communications network. But it is also the least efficient. If we had to drive to people to talk to them we would spend our whole life travelling. When we need to communicate with someone we write to them, send them a fax, or simply pick up the telephone. And the fastest way of communicating is the Internet.

Theoretically, the Internet should be as pervasive as the telephone network. As the world becomes more comfortable with the personal computer and the nature of Internet access changes, we will witness a new era in communications.

When someone says to you, "Just e-mail me the invitation," you won't return with, "E-mail, what do you mean?"

If someone said to you "fax me the details" ten years ago you may have got a similar response. But the fax is now an acceptable form of communication and those who have not embraced it by now must have a lot of time on their hands (because they are hand-delivering everything).

The telephone *is* the real information superhighway. Because at this point in time most people accept it as a medium and most use it. No one ever looks at you with a high-tech sense of fear if you say, "call me later ...". But many people have yet to browse the Web, let alone send e-mail. The telephone is accessible. Public telephones are the first choice in communications for the world traveller, and it is with this technology that people run their lives. Appointments, business transactions and relationships are all executed using the telephone network. But this is changing. People will take as much as they can get, given the opportunity to communicate more efficiently.

Now that the world has become more comfortable with computers and the Internet we are witnessing a new era in communications, as everything these days is being done digitally. Focus is on efficiency and speed. Time is the most precious commodity we have, and the Internet saves us plenty of it.

Digital diversions

In the past five years we have travelled, virtually, via undersea fibre optic cabling, exploring new cultures and artificial realities. The digital world of the Internet has as its basic communications elements, not a natural language (like English), but bits – binary numbers that flow in all directions. These binary numbers carry stories, and feelings, and great excitement. Our journey into cyberspace is digital by definition only. At a human level it is the most expressive medium we have seen to date. A cyber-medium that allows us to dream and create magic like never before. So, the next time you go window shopping, remember that there is a virtual alternative. It is called "windows shopping" and the place it happens is called cyberspace – the ultimate in trading spaces.

Computers are generic machines. In other words they can perform almost limitless functions, from simple mathematical calculations to intricate special effects, all at literally the tap of a key (or combination of keys). They can create special effects relatively inexpensively, with a degree of accuracy and detail which would be impossible to re-create any other way. This leads us to a current computer buzzword – *virtual*. A computer is a generic and a virtual machine. Your computer screen is a virtual desktop impersonating an actual desktop (and it's probably much tidier than the real thing too).

Unlike other machines, computers can execute a practically infinite number of software programs. One minute you have a word processor, the next a financial management tool, and then an arcade game. This concept of a series of virtual machines is what differentiates computers from other machines. A car is always a car, a television is always a television, a microwave is always a microwave (except when it's a virtual tumble dryer, drying out your last pair of socks). These machines all serve a *specific* function, so they are not virtual machines. They are physical workhorses that allow you to communicate, travel, work, and live. A computer, on the other hand, is a *collection* of virtual workhorses – an entire world of digital helpers living in a box.

The computer has an almost unlimited number of virtual applications. For example, it can become a virtual television set, showing your favourite shows. Yet the traditional television set cannot become a computer because you can't program it to create virtual applications. Television is not interactive – you cannot participate in its programmes. It is this participation which is the key element in computing, because no matter what you think, computers can't! People often marvel at the brilliance of a computer, forgetting that a human being had to invent a program and store it in the computer's memory before it could do anything at all. Computers obey commands, and although they have the potential to run numerous and various applications, these applications are people-generated.

People are often intimidated by computers because they can't believe that a machine can perform such mind-boggling feats. This fear of the new and unknown should not prevent anyone from enjoying computers. It is not necessary to understand the technology involved in the manufacture and programming of computers. Farmers don't need to know the intricate mechanical workings of their combine harvesters – they need to know how to use them efficiently to work their land. These days computer interfaces have advanced to a level of extreme user-friendliness. Microsoft's Windows operating system consists of graphic representations that are not much more than common sense. You don't need to learn a whole new "computer language" to operate a computer – if you can read, you can perform computerised tasks.

Technology has caused considerable anxiety throughout history, yet its aim has always been the same – to improve on previous methods. Computers are machines that have advanced to such an extent that they have begun not only to usurp jobs from "mere mortals", but also from other fellow machines. No matter what it is about computers that fascinates or horrifies you, you can't ignore the fact that everything we do converges within the space of the computer screen. This convergence towards digital machines has resulted in the Internet.

An internet is a network of networks. The global telephone system is a telephone internet. The global postal service is a postal internet.

Hey, you may have just realised that you have in fact been an internet user for many years now.

A PABX, or telephone switchboard, is a network. All the

telephones in the world make up an internet of PABXs and domestic stand-alone telephones. Like a computer network or Local Area Network (LAN), a PABX consists of electronic terminals that are all inter-connected. Each telephone on a PABX network has a unique address – a phone number – and the network represents a way of communicating between these addresses through speech.

A PABX gives us an alternative infrastructure for communications in the office environment. Why walk to the other side of the building when you can simply pick up the phone? It isn't so bad walking across the hall to tell someone something. After all, e-mail has never helped anyone stay in shape. With e-mail we let our fingers do the walking. There's no exercise in that. We need to let our legs do the walking occasionally. Instead, our fingers are doing the talking. Hey, this is getting confusing. Yes, we are doing it digitally, but are we progressing?

The telephone allows for vertical living and working. The Internet takes this one step beyond. Everything that applies to the physical world has a direct counterpart in the virtual world of cyberspace.

[Six]

There is an ISP in your future ...

The Internet is a lot like sex. Everyone's talking about it but no one wants to pay for it. Like sex, the Internet is something you are going to get at some point in time. The only question is: who are you going to get it from? Ah, that's where ISPs come into the equation. When you do eventually get it, remember to practise safe networking. The last thing you want is to get screwed online. Yes, there is going to be an ISP in your future. So, let's see what ISPs are all about.

An Internet Service Provider (ISP) is a company that connects people to the Internet. The first commercial ISPs started appearing in 1993 all around the globe. Our company was one of them. Today, IS spans a vast range of disciplines, from custom software development, to Web site construction, to secure transaction processing, to legacy system integration, to firewalling, to training, to intranet and extranet deployment. There are, in fact, more than thirty distinct services that our company now offers, and we can only imagine that this is going to continue expanding as the virtual landscape keeps on changing and evolving.

All of the services that ISPs provide are a consequence of a wired world. The systems these organisations build are focused around online distributed systems. Connecting people to the Internet will always be an important mission, because without a

The real voyage of **discovery** comes not in seeking new landscapes but in **having new eyes**.

Marcel Proust

virtual community there will be no one to enjoy the fruits of our continuing developments. The more people online, the better. Like a shopping centre, critical mass is a strategic imperative. Everybody benefits from greater choice, and the Internet is no different. ISPs around the world are all growing at overwhelmingly fast rates due to the increasing demand for connectivity. Successful ISPs are demonstrating incredible agility by continually re-inventing themselves as new age electronic commerce facilitators. Our company continues to change at a nerve-wracking pace as we adapt to emerging trends in online business.

There are two different Internet markets: the domestic or SOHO (Small Office Home Office) market and the corporate market. The domestic market is characterised by stand-alone PCs and modems whereas the corporate market is made up of LANs (Local Area Network) connected permanently to ISPs via routers and high-speed digital leased lines. The Internet market is similar to the telephone arena which has two unique sectors: the home users with stand-alone phone instruments and the corporate market with PABXs (switchboards).

The services offered to the home market are quite straightforward. Connectivity is via a modem and flat-rates are the most popular pricing models throughout the world. ISPs in this arena distinguish themselves by such things as modem-user ratios (the more modems per user the better), help-desk facilities (nothing is worse than being a frustrated first-time user), value-added services (Usenet news, free Web space, mail aliases, roaming, content, chat rooms, etc.), price, speed of access, and so on.

The corporate market is very different. Like the telephone market, the stand-alone home user has a very simple service with a clear set of parameters. The PABX market, on the other hand, involves a whole suite of services that generally require consultation and specific on-going support and expertise. A modern switchboard typically provides service for tele-sales, call centres, corporate voice mail, call forwarding, DID facilitation, caller ID, call logging, call barring, and so on. The corporate Internet market is simply taking this one step beyond. ISPs that have survived until this point are multifaceted organisations that employ consultants,

You **never**
close a sale,
you open a
long term
relationship.

Theodore Levitt

engineers, software developers, graphic artists, project managers, sales people, strategic thinkers, analysts, system architects, database programmers, server administrators, and so on. This big melting pot of differing talents is responsible for building online worlds in the areas of banking, publishing, broking, retailing, education, information sharing, etc.

The buck stops here

Holistic or turnkey solutions are what companies want. They want to minimise their exposure and maximise their return on their IT investment. In short, they want one-stop Internet shopping. Nowadays, the leading ISPs around the world have the ability to integrate their core competencies and provide a turnkey service - this is one of the primary reasons our organisation has succeeded thus far. Just think about it: a company can go to so many different Internet suppliers for so many different types of services. They can go to supplier A for leased line access, supplier B for a firewall, supplier C for Web site design, supplier D for dial-up access, supplier E for legacy system integration, supplier F for business consulting, supplier G for content delivery, supplier H for intranet construction, supplier I for application software development, supplier J for training, supplier K for Web hosting, supplier L for virtual private networking, and so on. Or they can choose a one-stop Internet supplier and save a lot of time. ISPs that are leading the industry offer a definite value proposition that is holistic in nature.

Imagine dealing with a different supplier for each type of Internet service. The cost of managing relationships with so many different suppliers would be incredibly restrictive on one's resources. The time you would need to invest in forming so many relationships with so many suppliers would also be very expensive. Today, corporate ISPs who are succeeding in the corporate market are diversified organisations that bring together many different disciplines under one roof. ISPs have the ability to become powerful, global consulting firms with a strong technical focus, as more and more IT initiatives converge around the online world.

It is no wonder that ISPs are very stressful organisations to

*To believe
       is very dull.
To doubt
       is intensely engrossing.*

Oscar Wilde

work for. Our company operates at a pace that is unparalleled. The pressures brought about by continuous change can be quite hard to cope with. One of the reasons we wrote this book is because we have lived over 10 years in just under 5 in the ISP industry. We have made a lot of mistakes in that time. But we have also done some amazing things. We have built a company that is exciting, innovative and humming with energy. One thing that will certainly always be a frustration is the fact that everyone is quick to blame their ISP. There is much knowledge still to be shared with the world on the subject of computers and networking.

The ISP business is very intriguing. Everyone wants in. But the infrastructure costs will paralyse you, the hours will kill you, and if you still have some strength at the end of day then someone will find you and blame you for something you never ever did.

Everyone always blames their ISP

Personal computing is a lot like motoring. There are many different models, with many options. There are many suppliers. One person sells you the car, another one installs the radio, another fits the mag wheels, and another one installs the car phone. Still another group of companies sells you the petrol and, finally, a mysterious organisation provides us with the roads. Computing is even more fascinating. We buy PCs from shops that are often no longer in business a year later. We buy modems somewhere else. We buy software from, er, there is not much choice here, from Bill. We get Internet access from different ISPs. The phone line is supplied by the telephone company. That is where computing and motoring go their separate ways. When your car phone breaks you know who to go and see. When your car backfires you know who to call. So why is it when your word processor locks up, or your PC reboots, or your modem just hangs, you call your ISP and make it their problem?

You can contrast this scenario to the television world. When TV first made its debut there was not much to watch. Then pay TV operators launched their offerings and suddenly the TV was being used more and more. This led to many more TVs being sold, and many more TVs breaking down and getting repaired. But when your TV goes on the blink you don't phone your cable TV company. You call your friendly neighbourhood TV repair shop. You don't blame the pay TV operator for your television breaking down. But they have caused you to use it more, so indirectly that helped it become old and tired as it gets put through its paces with all the different channels these days. This is what the Internet has done to personal computers. So please, stop blaming your friendly ISP when you lose a file, or when your disk drive crashes.

We would like to share with you a short story at this point. An urban legend that is used around these parts to illustrate the position that awaits us each working day. It is a wonderful tale which we heard from one of our colleagues here at work, and it is right on the money. It goes something like this ... as with most countries in the world, Zimbabwe is experiencing a resurgence of religious fundamentalism. One day the Harare central post office receives an envelope addressed only to "God" with no return address or other markings. As they have no way of delivering the mail they decide to open the envelope. On doing this they discover what must be the saddest letter you have ever read:

Mrs Mthembu
101 West Street
Bulawayo
Zimbabwe

Dear God,

My children and I are starving, I have been unemployed for several months now and simply cannot get ahead. If only you could let me have $100 I could get back on my feet again.

Sincerely,
Mrs Mthembu

The good people of the post office simply couldn't let this suffering continue so they held a collection and, believe it or not, after emptying the change from everyone's pockets they only managed to scrape together $99. Nevertheless, they wrote a covering letter in return:

> Dear Mrs Mthembu,
>
> I am deeply saddened to hear of your plight, enclosed please find the money you requested.
>
> I hope you get back on your feet soon.
>
> Sincerely,
> God

A few weeks later another letter arrives at the Harare post office marked, as before, with "God" only. Once again the good citizens employed at the post office open the letter and inside they find:

> Dear God,
>
> Thank you so much for the money you sent. It has just about enabled my children and I to get back on our feet again. Now if only those bastards at the post office hadn't stolen a dollar ...

Why does everyone blame the post office? I guess it is in the same way that everyone blames their ISP when an important document goes missing, or when their PC freezes up at a critical moment. Let us tell you why the Internet is causing all these sudden acts of frustration. Well, there is only one real reason: the Net has made computing hip. Suddenly, everyone is buying PCs. Our digital workhorses are starting to run at full gallop. Yes, people are using their computers more and more. Because there is so much going on in the virtual world.

Compare an ISP to a car dealer. Imagine going to see the

local car lot and telling the salesman "I want some good reasons why I should drive". If the salesman has not disappeared by then, go ahead and say "Ok, I'm convinced ... now teach me to drive." If the salesman is still around after that one, go on and say "Very well ... now where can I go with my new car ... give me ten good destinations to take my kids this weekend." Now, stop for a minute, and think. Imagine using the same dialogue with an ISP. This is what happens so often. People want to know why the Internet is going to be beneficial to them. Then they want you to teach them how to drive a PC. Then they say, "So, where are the good Web sites".

Think about the very early years of the car – which weren't terribly different, by way of both contrast and comparison. Did early car dealers have to supply road maps? What about tourist brochures? Cars represented a new way of life, and a new challenge. The Internet too represents a new way of life. ISPs have to add value to the medium as well as spell out the destinations. The challenge, though, is far greater; at no other time in the history of the world has the rate of change been so intense. Yes, everything is changing so fast.

It does sound a little crazy, but it is quite understandable. The Internet has grown incredibly fast, and in doing so, has begun to transform the way people talk, live, work, shop and play. It isn't as bad as it used to be in 1993 though. There is so much more media coverage around the online world that people are pretty wired these days. Internet literacy is on the up and up and people are beginning to understand the Internet at a grassroots level. But still, we do get blamed for those digital dilemmas that face you, and all of us, each day. Please try to understand, we are here to help. Don't fight with us when your power supply catches fire.

Intruder alert, intruder alert !!!

One of the biggest areas of opportunity is around network security. There is still much misinformation out there and this has led to many security innovations. The concern for online security is justified, as financial institutions and retailers connect their mighty legacy systems to the Net in an attempt to streamline their offerings and enhance their businesses. But this leaves them exposed to hackers – who are forever lurking in cyberspace – waiting to take advantage of a vulnerable system, often just for the challenge of it. Like jumbo shrimp, military intelligence, or parliamentary action, network security is an oxymoron – two words that appear to contradict each other. But this contradiction stems from a stubborn, historical mind-set that needs to be debunked.

The problem with securing any machine connected to a computer network is that of entropy. Even though the machine itself may not change, its security will gradually weaken as more and more people become aware of that machine's existence; and as previously undiscovered flaws in the hardware, software, or manner in which the machine was secured, come to light. System administrators may also find it difficult to implement a security policy consistently on those machines which have to cater for a large variety of user needs. It is not uncommon to find notoriously insecure software packages being run on mission-critical machines. In fact, the users themselves can be responsible for leaving a system wide open to attack through poorly chosen passwords or indiscriminate resource sharing. Firewalls provide a convenient means of securing an entire network from a particular avenue of attack.

A firewall generally consists of several components designed to moderate traffic between two networks (namely, your network and the Internet). Firewalls are intended to restrict access to internal (and possible external) machines on the basis of who is trying to use them, and from where. Firewalls offer many advantages, not the least of which is a single point of disconnection from the outside – a desperate but effective measure. In addition, a good firewall should have the following features: all traffic from inside your company to the outside world, and vice versa, must pass through the firewall; only authorised traffic, as defined by your company's security policy, should be allowed to pass through; and the firewall itself should be immune to any unauthorised penetration.

The key to your network's safety lies in defining a company-wide security policy. It is generally a good idea to have a concrete goal in mind when undertaking the securing of a network. Two main questions need to be answered: What resources need to be protected and against whom? A firewall is the obvious solution when it's desirable to protect all of the resources on the network. Otherwise securing individual computers on the network may suffice.

The second question is: against whom do these resources need to be protected? The sophistication of an attacker who may attempt to gain access to your organisation's network will influence the choice of security measures. A simple packet filter on external routers may prevent casual attempts to penetrate your network, but is unlikely to thwart a determined assault by a hacker.

It must be stressed that a firewall is only an implementation of a more general security policy. The installation of a firewall on an Internet connection, for example, does not guarantee that your network will not be compromised from another source (internal modems, connections to other networks, etc.). Above all, a firewall should not be seen as an excuse to relax the security of a network protected by the firewall.

It is safe to say that your network's security is no laughing matter (no joke intended). So, practise safe networking. One of the main reasons that large companies roll out firewalls is to manage Internet usage. ISPs have assisted many corporations to understand who in their organisation is using the Internet, when they are using it, and what for. In the same way that companies don't want their members to knock up huge international phone bills, they also don't want them wasting valuable business time looking at dirty pictures on the Net.

Viva virtual

ISPs represent a base of users which can be called a virtual community. This community represents a critical mass of users that are searching for value in the virtual world. ISPs in collaboration with traditional retailers are trying to provide this value by giving people what they want: more convenient shopping for goods and service, and more effective communications between the members of the online community.

"Virtual Private Networks" (VPN) is one of the latest buzz-phrases. Intranets made a big noise in 1998, but 1999 looks as if it will be remembered in technology circles as the year of the VPN.

A private digital computer network is formed by establishing a permanent online circuit between any two points. If, for example, a bank connects its head office to the stock exchange via a digital leased line (supplied by the telephone company) then a private WAN (Wide Area Network) has in effect been constructed. Companies have been connecting their LANs (Local Area Network) together for years. Networking vendors have made a lot of money selling computer networking infrastructure. Of course, software firms like Microsoft and Novell have also made money selling distributed software applications that run across these networks. But not everyone can afford to construct their own private networks. Not everyone wants to. Before you know it, you have a large network centre, a few dozen computer engineers on your payroll, and a fortune in digital machinery that depreciates at the speed of light. You start by installing a WAN link to your auditors for more efficient financial assistance, then you connect to your IT suppliers for faster online support, and of course you need to communicate with your advertising agency quickly in these fast-changing times, and before you know it, you have a big network infrastructure to maintain. Did someone say Internet?

The Internet is about sharing infrastructure. When a company connects its network to the Internet it can communicate with all the other organisations on this global communications medium. One link. One network. But there is also one problem. The Internet is an open, uncontrolled infrastructure that is not private. A private network is exactly that – free of outsiders. So the question is: how do you construct a network that exploits cost-effective common infrastructure (like the Internet) in such a way that your communications remain private, with guaranteed service levels? Today's financial institutions specifically need secure computer communications with predictable response times and service level agreements due to the sensitive nature of the transactions they process. Time is money and no one understands this better than banks, stockbrokers and insurance giants. An efficient, consistent digital infrastructure is what they need to make them global giants.

Private networking provides you with the peace of mind required. You control your network and hence accountability is straightforward. But the costs become significant and, before you know it, your company's IT department becomes a big entity in its own right. It is in this space that global giants like EDS and *debis* were born. Sharing infrastructure by exploiting communication channels like the Internet is the way to go.

The question is: how does one utilise a shared network and achieve the desired comfort zones that are so very necessary for today's global leaders? VPNs can be created by utilising Frame-Relay switching technology to construct "virtual tunnels" that run across specific points on the Internet. ISPs with big communities can leverage their market share which relates to a concentration point of common business partners. In South Africa, IS, for example, can leverage its big corporate market share to the benefit of all its clients. IS' virtual community connects the country's leading financial institutions, media houses, advertising agencies, auditing firms, IT suppliers, and so on. Any modern corporation can use this virtual real-estate to its advantage by connecting to it, and by creating a virtual traffic circle that allows inter-connectivity amongst suppliers, customers and business partners.

An ISP can provide a safe, predictable inter-connection point for all the members of its community. Apart from communicating with all the other parties on the Internet, the members of an online community can construct a virtual private network that has guaranteed information transfer rates or CIRs (Committed Information Rates) by exploiting Frame-Relay switching across an ISP's backbone. For example, if a media house and an advertising agency both connect to a specific ISP, then those two companies could construct virtual tunnels between them facilitated by the ISP in the middle to exchange, for example, advertising material. Market share is everything in this virtual community. Just think of the people you do business with – how many of them are on the Internet? Surely this can be utilised to the maximum benefit of all concerned. Everyone wins in this day and age where we continually strive for faster, more efficient forms of digital communications.

This may not be an easy scenario to comprehend. VPN services represent a new phenomenon, and there are many kinds of VPNs. Here we are referring to a VPN that can be constructed by leveraging the critical mass of an established ISP. Yes, market share in this case relates to a community. And a community needs to communicate. The local mall is an example of critical mass in the physical world. It represents a concentration of shoppers, and in simpler terms, traffic. The local mall is always very busy – it has a lot of traffic. This is why everyone wants to have their shops situated there. You wouldn't build your superstore in the middle of the desert. Virtual communities represent the same ideal – look for them in the world's ISPs, they are there for you, waiting to be exploited. Remember, everyone scores in this mathematical wonderland because, after all, it is the people of cyberspace who make it what it is. The more people online, the more you can do. Simple.

Change change change

The greatest challenge that an ISP has to face is its ability to re-invent itself continuously. The Internet landscape is continually changing as the envelope is pushed further and further in terms of what technology allows us to do. Furthermore, the virtual community is becoming increasingly more receptive to online shopping and this is creating tremendous momentum in the e-commerce arena. Agility is key here as ISPs face a continuous discontinuity because technology and consumer paradigms just keep shifting and shifting.

This constant change has caused many Internet orientated companies to become pressure cookers, with stress levels set at unprecedented levels. ISPs that do not adapt get usurped by wave after wave of upstarts who identified a new paradigm and launched ship. It has not been an easy five years for us in the Internet industry, but it has been very exciting. We have seen many people burn-out, and we have seen many skilled people become obsolete because they have not embraced new trends. Those who dare, win, in this high-tech race that constantly changes course at increasingly faster and faster rates.

With a view to our group's strategy, we firmly believe that

our business model should be to expand globally via network service provision and distributed software integration initiatives. Our ultimate objective is to be global enablers of e-commerce. This strategy has evolved over a period of time and is under constant development and exploration.

It is important to see that the great companies of the world, the great companies in the IT industry, such as IBM, Hewlett-Packard and Microsoft have had the ability to reinvent themselves continuously. The one constant that we face is that change is what IT is all about. We continually have to strive to identify new markets and nurture people to think differently. If we are able to do that, and if we have energy, breadth and vision, we will continue to grow and be a successful company.

The world's telecommunications, media and traditional IT firms are all converging as alliances are constantly being formed across the globe. No one knows ultimately where to position themselves in the virtual world, so partnerships are being established as companies pool their resources in an effort to catch the massive pot of gold at the end of the fibre optic rainbow. We can only imagine that things are going to be a lot more stressful before some solid foundations are laid. Again, we are going to go forward and backward all at once. The progress paradox has us all running around in so many directions, pioneering and innovating so much new ground, while living less and less. Time is the one luxury that ISP men and women are not finding in abundance in this new world that is moving at the speed of light.

The more people online, the better. As in a shopping centre, critical mass is a strategic imperative. Everybody benefits from greater choice. The Internet is no different. It is the people of cyberspace who make it what it is. The more people online, the more you can do.

[Seven]

What's in a name?

Internet domain names have become a topic for serious discussion, with battles being waged in the world's courtrooms in an effort to secure the ownership of tradenames in cyberspace. In case you were wondering, a domain name is that label which binds your organisation to just about everything it does online (from an e-mail address to your Web site). Some familiar domain names include: playboy.com, microsoft.com, ananzi.co.za, nedbank.co.za, and mcdonalds.com. In fact, the McDonald's story of how a large global player had to fight to control its name on the Net is a famous tale by now. It may sound silly, it may even seem childish, but the Internet is not a country, and its inhabitants are not governed by any particular business policies. When you start a company in the physical world you typically register a name for your business, and perhaps you even apply for various trademarks to be protected world-wide, but in cyberspace it's a free for all. Yup, it's first come first served.

Some companies have moved fast and registered a domain name for later use. Other organisations are actively using theirs as you read this. Some corporations are embroiled in frustrating legal battles trying to claim theirs back. McDonald's is such a company that won their fight. But what is the real problem? In theory there are infinite domain names to go around, but in practice people are uninformed and more often than not, scared into a corner, especially when it comes to the ".com" suffix. The online world has many suffixes you can choose from when registering a domain name for your organisation. In South Africa, for example, the vast majority of companies have chosen to register themselves in the "co.za" (commercial South Africa) domain space, as in, liberty.co.za, fnb.co.za, and bmw.co.za. The ".com" domain space is characteristic of America. But these are just conventions. They are not rules. If Acme Widgets wants to register the name acme.com then all they have to do is check whether that name is available, and, presto, it can be theirs with some simple procedures.

Do not panic if the ".com" name is not available for your organisation. If your business is South African, for example, then the "co.za" domain space is more than perfect. If you manage to get ".com" as well, then that is also fine. Think about this: all American phone numbers start with the prefix "555" (well, at least this is the case on television). Does your South African phone number start with "555"? Do we have to be so American all the time? If someone tries to extort money from you abroad by telling you that they have registered your company's name in ".com" and if you want it back you need to cough up, then tell them to stick it. There are always alternatives. And if someone has deliberately registered your South African corporation's name in "co.za" and is playing hardball, then the chances are they are based in South Africa, so get in your car and go give them a hiding. If someone purposefully copied your logo or company's name in the physical world then you would take action. The same goes for the virtual world.

To avoid headaches get in early – register a domain name for your company and secure your identity online now before someone else nabs it. Domain sharks are out there, waiting to extort money from you in return for your name – so, beat them to it: register your organisation's domain name and relax. Even if you only plan to launch a Web site in the future, and even if you only plan to communicate online years from now, rather be safe than sorry. You are particularly at risk if your trademark has a generic make-up. For example, if a company is called the Golden Bus Corporation then there is a good chance that domains like golden.com and golden.co.za are already taken. Who the true custodian of the name "Golden" is, is an interesting debate. In the offline world, your trademark represents your identity in the marketplace, making your products recognisable for the people you do business with, particularly your customers. On the Net, domain names have come to fulfil the same role as a trademark.

A domain name identifies your company online. It represents a symbol of goodwill online. Generally, domain names are assigned on a first come first served basis by various regional entities who have been given the responsibility of domain name registration. These registrars do not exercise power over a requested name – as long as that name does not already exist you can have it. In theory, this means that anyone can register a domain that belongs to a well known and established trademark, or proprietary name, that exists in the offline world. However, in the United States, for example, this situation has often been remedied in practice by the courts, as in the case of MTV – the domain name hijackers had no legitimate purpose for obtaining these domain names and they were ordered to hand them back to their rightful custodians. There is no clear cut law in this regard; trademark violations and uncompetitive practices are real challenges to the system.

What's in a domain name system?

One of the key success factors behind the Internet is entrenched in the Domain Name System (DNS). DNS is a distributed database which is always there, working in the background, mapping names to numbers, so that your journey through cyberspace is as easy as point and click. DNS is not a new phenomenon – the Americans have been using this concept with telephone numbers for years. When you see an advert in the US that says something like "For a good time dial 1-800-H-O-T-S-E-X" this is simply domain name mapping in action. The name is mapped to a number when you make the call. Check out your phone a little closer, the "1" has "abc" the "2" has "def" on it, and so on. Mapping names to numbers is brilliant. It is easy to remember a name. And that is why a domain name is so important.

DNS liberates us from numeric information, in much the same way as street names and numbers shield us from longitude and latitude. A domain name system is a generic application. It is evident in various manifestations on traditional communications infrastructures (networks) – we have in fact been using "DNS" for many many years, because it is far easier to remember a name than some unrepresentative string of digits. DNS is the key to all the applications' (software) ease of use across the Internet. An Internet user does not need to worry about how DNS works, but just be conscious that it exists.

DNS maps names into numbers, and humans remember words better than digits. But memory is not the only advantage. One can formulate addresses much more easily in words using intuition and guesswork. One cannot guess a company's telephone number, or their postal address, or physical address, for that matter. But guessing a Web address (URL) can be quite intuitive.

Client-server is the name of the game

Each Internet application (e-mail, WWW, Usenet news, ftp, etc.) is based on the idea of client-server computing, which allows multiple clients or customers to concurrently utilise a server or service. Contrast this with the telephone whereby once you are engaged in conversation, you are just that, engaged. This is a clear limitation of one-to-one relations characteristic of current telephony. A "client" is a software program that is used to access a "server" software program. Many clients can access a server at the same time (i.e., concurrency is the norm). In this fashion, an online shop, or a Web server, can be simultaneously browsed and manipulated by people all over the world who are using Web client software programs (the most popular Web software programs or clients are Netscape Navigator and Microsoft Internet Explorer). Think of a client software program as the customer, and a server software program as the service. In this light it is clear that many customers can shop at one particular service simultaneously, and even talk to other customers who are in the shop at the same time. Each of these virtual shops has an Internet address or URL (Universal Resource

Locator) which companies are putting on their business cards, letterheads, billboards, newspaper adverts and television and radio commercials. These online shops can be accessed by the online community 24 hours a day.

Technically, each Internet client-server application is based on a protocol used for communication between the client and the server. For example, SMTP (Simple Mail Transfer Protocol) is used by a mail program (typically found on a PC or Mac) to send and receive e-mail from an e-mail server or post office (typically found on a UNIX machine or Windows NT). Associated with each server or service is an address – you simply connect to the address of the service that you wish to utilise. When you send mail for example, you in fact send a message to a person at an electronic post office, or a mail server, which has an address. As with other infrastructures, all addresses on the Internet are unique. Each shop, bank, postal box, library, etc. has a unique Internet address. The only difference between an Internet address and addresses found on other infrastructures, is that an Internet address makes sense. Our company's telephone number in Johannesburg is 283-5000; where this number came from is still a mystery. The telephone company dreams it up and presto! But the online shop from Coca-Cola, say, can be found at www.cocacola.com (or www.coke.com). This is simply the Web site address for the commercial organisation Coca-Cola. Much easier to remember and much easier to guess. Now try to guess Coca-Cola's telephone number in America!

You name it

E-mail addresses are popping up on business cards, television commercials, and magazines all across the globe. Instead of writing to someone at a PO Box, people are typing electronic mail messages to business associates, customers, suppliers and friends, and delivering them all over the world in practically no time at all, without regard for costs (there are no postage stamps to worry about). The benefits are numerous, but once again the most valuable is the saving in time. DNS makes this way of life possible. Internet addresses are easy to remember and easy to formulate.

E-mail and postal mail are synonymous as they share the same generic protocols and perform the same functions. The purpose of both is to communicate with another person who is not in the immediate vicinity. Letter writing ranges from the crumpled up notes thrown between school children during a boring lesson (compared to Internet training that is), to keeping in contact with a person overseas, to corporate business correspondence. Every letter must have the name of the recipient, an address and a stamp. E-mail is the same. In order to send e-mail the requirements include a user name and domain name (these together constitute an e-mail address), for example, bill@microsoft.com. The recipient's name comes before the "@" (pronounced "at") symbol followed by the domain name of the organisation. And yes, there are no stamps. Instead you need a $3000 computer. Go figure. Are we really progressing?

Just name the place, er, space

Once you are up and running, where do you go? Navigating your way around the Internet can be intimidating at first. There are so many places, er, spaces to visit, so many cultures to experience, and so many exciting things on offer. But as you get familiar with the enabling tools i.e. your Web browser, and your e-mail programme, you will start to treat the Internet like a new car – you use it when you need to commute. When you buy a car for the first time there is the thrill of being mobile and you literally go surfing along the freeways and through the lanes and alleyways of your neighbourhood. But then the novelty wears off and the joy-rides begin to cease as you realise the car is simply an enabling technology. It enables you to commute, and ultimately, to get things done. Without the car you would be stuck. Without the Internet you will be stuck too – stuck in one place that is. When you joy-ride in your car you do it in a local area (i.e. your surrounding neighbourhood). It is simply too far to drive to London (when you live in Johannesburg that is). The Internet changes all that because everything online is a single mouse click away. The Internet allows you to explore new areas that, before you got connected, were always too far away.

When you get a car, or a telephone, or a fax, you never ask, "Ok, I can use this – but where do I begin?" Often people get lost in cyberspace, or they just don't know where to begin. The point is (like the car or telephone for example) there is no starting point. No one ever said to their car dealer "Ok, I can drive and its great ... now, can you tell me where I can go?" No one ever phoned their phone company and said "The phone is amazing ... now give me a number to call".

ISPs are constantly being asked for such information by new Netizens who are also frantically buying books of Internet addresses – there are so many "Yellow Pages" for the Internet for sale in bookshops these days. You don't phone people for the sake of phoning (okay, occasionally you phone someone just to shoot the breeze), and in the same light you don't surf the Net for the sake of surfing. But you will explore it initially and, ultimately, it will be a communications tool.

The roads have map books. The telephone has the infamous "Yellow Pages". What does the Internet have? Online we call them search engines or directories and two of the best examples of these are Yahoo! and Lycos. These are global Internet directories where people list their Web sites so that you can find them easily (literally with the click of a mouse). As the Internet gains more and more global acceptance (i.e. as it grows outside the US) there will be more need for localised information pertaining to a specific region. This is already evident as territorial search engines have emerged all over the place. In South Africa, the Ananzi search engine (www.ananzi.co.za) is a prime example of such a service – Ananzi only serves information about South African Web sites.

The cheque is in the e-mail

A typical Internet address (i.e. an e-mail address) may look something like ronnie@is.co.za for example. Compare a traditional postal snail mail address (commonly called this on the Net because it takes so long to arrive) with an Internet address and you will notice some similarities. They both address a person, in this example "Ronnie", at a place (in the physical world) and a space (in the virtual world) – "Ronnie" has a post box on the physical roads infrastructure (one can also have a PO Box at a post office) and an online post box on the Internet. The physical postal address describes a street name, a suburb, a postal code (which is meant as a more efficient alternative to the suburb) and a country name. The Internet e-mail address (ronnie@is.co.za) includes an organisation's name ("is" for The Internet Solution), a description of what sector this organisation is in ("co" for the commercial sector), and a country code ("za" for South Africa). Snail mail can take the form of a post box at one's home or a PO Box offered by a post office.

Using a communications infrastructure requires knowledge of how to formulate addresses and of usage protocols. When you use the telephone, for example, you need to know how to dial, how to conduct yourself online (on the telephone line that is), what to expect (don't expect to find Bill Gates by calling Microsoft in Seattle), and, most importantly, you need to know the telephone number to ring. The same goes for the Internet. You need to know how to use an e-mail program, how to conduct yourself (this is called netiquette), what to expect (don't expect Bill to e-mail you back in a hurry), and you need to know the e-mail address you want to send a message to. Like snail mail, don't expect to find any cheques in your e-mail (at least not yet ... although e-cheques are around the corner).

Netiquette, or network etiquette, describes the online culture – the way Internet users communicate. Think of netiquette as the "dos" and "don'ts" of cyberspace. Lower case letters and shortforms r acceptable, but UPPER CASE means you are raising your voice. And a smiley like this :-) depicts a happy face. So, try 2 b a gr8 netizen ;-).

The domain difference

Each country (other than the US) typically has a two letter suffix associated with its domain. For example "uk" is for the United Kingdom, "de" is for Germany, and "za" is for South Africa. The next part of the domain name is also characteristic, with "co" representing the commercial or corporate and "ac" signifying the academic arena, as in, uct.ac.za, for the University of Cape Town. The Americans had to be different and opted for ".com". This is par for the course. They have different voltages, different TV standards, and they drive on the wrong side of the road. So, why should they conform now when it comes to cyberspace? But remember, these are just guidelines or conventions. Some companies in South Africa have registered themselves in ".com" as well as "co.za", for example, sasol.com and oldmutual.com.

Examples of Domain Names

Domain Name (example)	Domain Suffix	Domain Type
playboy.com	com	commercial in the US
anc.org.za	org.za	non-profit in SA
stanford.edu	edu	educational in the US
cam.ac.uk	ac.uk	educational in the UK
bt.co.uk	co.uk	commercial in the UK
siemens.de	de	organisation in Germany
nasa.gov	gov	government in the US
didata.co.za	co.za	commercial in SA
alcatel.fr	fr	organisation in France

In the US the original domain name space included .EDU (education), .COM (commercial), .GOV (government), .MIL (military), .ORG (non-profit organisation), and .NET (network operator as in AT & T or MCI). A commercial organisation such as Walt Disney, for example, would have a domain registered in the .COM domain (disney.com), and a network operator such as Sprint would be in the .NET domain (sprint.net), and so on. The incredible growth of the Internet in the US resulted in numerous registrations in each of these domain spaces. As the rest of the world started to connect to the Net it was obvious that more domain name space was necessary and the result was the creation of territorial suffixes (.fr , .de , .za , .uk , .jp , etc.) for the different countries of the globe. Further information was added in many cases to represent commerce (.co) or academia (.ac) or, in some cases, the organisation's name is simply appended to the territorial suffix as in ferrari.it (the car manufacturer in Italy).

As you can see, it is very easy to develop insight into how to formulate an Internet address (domain name) because the rules are quite intuitive. Contrast this with telephone numbers – we know that most telephone numbers in large cities are 7 digits in length, but can you guess someone's telephone number? Telephone numbers are by no means intuitive.

While it is quite easy to guess an Internet domain name and the subsequent Web address, to learn of a specific e-mail address of an individual one would have to ask that person over the telephone say, or send mail to the postmaster asking them for the relevant information. For example, one could send e-mail to postmaster@is.co.za asking for the e-mail address of Joe Soap. In this case the postmaster would simply pass this information on to Joe Soap and reply to the e-mail request by saying "Our e-mail addresses are confidential. I have forwarded your message to Mr Soap who will contact you directly". Contrast this to snail mail whereby companies constantly send junk mail to such generic people in your company as "Marketing Manager" or "Stationery Buyer". These junk mailers don't even know the names of the people they are mailing. They are hoping the right person will get the envelope and call them back to make an appointment, or ultimately buy something.

In the same way, a PABX telephone system offers the same anonymity whereby calls are screened by a secretary who generally asks you things like "What is it in connection with?" especially when someone asks to speak to the managing director (who in this company is constantly getting calls from schemers and dreamers wanting to open cyber-playgrounds and high-tech restaurants). In the Microsoft example of bill@microsoft.com we simply took a guess. The mail does get through but we never get an answer (Bill is probably very busy).

Examples of WWW addresses and e-mail addresses

Organisation name	WWW address	e-mail address (example)
UCLA	www.ucla.edu	webmaster@ucla.edu
The Internet Solution	www.is.co.za	jem@is.co.za
IBM	www.ibm.com	postmaster@ibm.com
Reuters	www.reuters.com	info@reuters.com
Toyota	www.toyota.co.jp	webmaster@toyota.co.jp
CNN	www.cnn.com	postmaster@cnn.com
Library of Congress	www.loc.gov	info@loc.gov
Ogilvy & Mather	www.ogilvy.com	webmaster@ogilvy.com
Microsoft	www.microsoft.com	bill@microsoft.com

Knock knock

Guessing an Internet address (i.e. a domain name) generally requires some knowledge of the type of organisation that you are looking for online and where it is situated on the globe. Most are easy to guess but some are cryptic because short forms (abbreviations) are used in the domain name. IBM (which stands for International Business Machines) is simply ibm.com and very easy to guess. But Ogilvy & Mather on the other hand has the domain name ogilvy.com. Not so obvious but easy to have guessed nonetheless. The Internet Solution (South Africa's largest ISP) has the domain name is.co.za. This one is a little cryptic. If you knew that IS stands for The Internet Solution in South Africa then you would have guessed it right away but it is not that obvious. Some companies choose cryptic domain names on purpose because of network security paranoia – they don't want anyone to know they are online.

Military organisations, for example, tend to keep a low profile online. A domain name like icbms.mil would be a challenge to a zealous hacker, don't you think? You can imagine how paranoid the military can be and you can appreciate how tight security has to be in this regard. Yes, we doubt that the local nuclear facility will have a Web site with which you can play around.

Some organisations have deliberately chosen a new name to

brand a product online. Time Warner's Web site is a classic example of this. Their Pathfinder service (pathfinder.com) can be viewed as marketing a brand new service from Time Warner rather than as an augmentation of their physical offerings. Brand building on the Web is growing and growing and these days we are seeing many companies register domain names that reflect brands. In South Africa, for example, SA Breweries (with domain sab.co.za) have registered many of their brands as domains, such as castle.co.za, amstel.co.za, and so on.

Generally all e-mail post offices have various generic mail boxes like postmaster, info or webmaster (the person who looks after the Web site). One would generally contact the postmaster at a domain name to find out more information about the people who have e-mail addresses at that organisation. For example, one could mail postmaster@cnn.com and ask them for Ted Turner's e-mail address. These generic e-mail addresses are analogous to such titles as secretary, marketing manager or general manager in the physical world of buildings and offices. The reason is exactly the same: a company will always have a marketing manager and, although that person may change over time, the job function and title will remain. Not only that, a company may have several webmasters who take turns at receiving and answering e-mail.

We can source information from a Web site, request something, and even e-mail someone directly. We have so many new ways of communicating, and so many more people we can make contact with in the virtual world. But are we really progressing? Do you really want to communicate with some magic-mushroom enthusiast who has just made contact with an ancient civilisation? If this guy showed up at your house and wanted to hang out and chat you would call the cops. So, why is the Internet breaking down these boundaries? Perhaps it isn't really. Perhaps we are still just enjoying the novelty of this new medium. As more and more people realise that the same people who annoyed them on the telephone are simply now going to annoy them via e-mail, they will start treating the Net as just another communications tool. Yes, domain naming may be a step forward technically, but it does not mean that, because you can guess-mail someone (like Bill Gates for example), that they will necessarily mail you back. Life has not changed, technology has. Yes, there are so many people to talk, er, type to, but there is still not much to say, expect for something like "got 2 go ... type 2 u 2-morrow ... i hope u have a gr8 day ... O/O". Now that is progress; and Shakespeare would cringe.

Everything online is a mouse click away. The Internet allows you to explore new things which, before you got connected, were always too far away.

[Eight]

Windows shopping

We live and shop in two worlds these days. "Born to shop" will soon be re-written as "born to surf". We shop for clothes, food, financial services and airline tickets. There is nothing new about shopping but the methods of shopping are changing. And a digital change it is. We can get in our car and drive to the mall or we can call up a Web site and click away. Spatial environments, characterised by the World Wide Web, are the new virtual malls of the late 1990s, and they will be a dominant form of consumerism in the 21st century. We will buy goods and services on the Net and in the process we will interact with people, virtually, from diverse cultural backgrounds.

Businesses today face the challenge of "bricks and mortar" versus the virtual world. There is no better example than the banking industry. Virtual banks situated on the Web with no real assets other than cash are able to streamline the activities of emerging Internet users. The days of people walking into a bank to collect cash or transfer funds are coming to an end. We believe this to be true of any business: our business and yours. This new world order says, "Why do I have to physically go into a store when I could be shopping online? Why do I have to go to a bank to draw cash when I could download it onto a smartcard all from the comfort of my own home?"

If you do not **think** about the **future**, you cannot have one.

John Galsworthy

Living in space and place is terrific. It gives us a lot of mobility and far more freedom of choice. Not that we lacked choice before this digital revolution, but now everything the world has to offer in its entirety is that much more accessible. We can cross borders at the click of a mouse and we can deposit our hard earned money in a bank at the end of the world (wherever that is these days) if we choose. In fact, we can shop with a truly global perspective for better insurance premiums, banking facilities, goods and services. This global shift from window shopping to windows shopping (from place to space) is changing all shopping paradigms. Yet, with all this diversity, we still recommend that you order a pizza from a nearby restaurant. Otherwise the delivery charge from Federal Express may give you indigestion (and you may also die of hunger). Yes, shopping itself is not changing, but the way we spend our hard earned money certainly is.

People who go to malls generally own cars, and people who browse Web sites typically own computers. Think about it: market your goods to people who can afford to buy them. Sell them online! But make sure that the goods you want to sell online will move. It is no use selling, say, soft drinks online, because how will you get your goods to the public? Interestingly enough, companies like Coca-Cola and Kellogg have the most fantastic online offerings, although they never try to sell you a Coke or a bowl of cornflakes from the Web.

Coca-Cola is one example of a company whose products will never be sampled or sold online – you can't drink Coke from a computer – but their Web site is very exciting (www.coke.com). It offers a range of interactive services like competitions, financial reports, a history of the company, expansion plans, and nutritional information. **It has created an online awareness which increases and improves their position in the marketplace by investing in the marketspace.**

The Net is the place, er, the space to be. The citizens of cyberspace are typically doing pretty good. Shopping, for these folk, is a way of life. Consider that in South Africa, for example, there are no homeless people surfing the Web. When was the last time you saw a person sleeping on a park bench clutching a laptop? The fact is

You can **dream** when you are sleeping, but to make them come **true**, you need to be **awake**.

Author Unknown

people who use the Internet represent purchasing power. The new virtual shops that are springing up online desperately want these consumers to visit their shops. It's the demographics of this online population that are so desirable.

Banking, entertainment, media, insurance, property, financial, legal, medical and retail sectors are all scrambling to set up shop on the World Wide Web – the ultimate trading space. The Web introduces a new standard in electronic commerce and provides a stable, robust, secure and scaleable mechanism for the sale of goods and services. The consumer, however, is not yet entirely impressed, because there are still relatively few signs of interactive, personalised services in this 'world within a world'. But that is all changing, and it is changing fast.

Worlds within worlds

Every business today competes in two worlds: physical (the marketplace) and virtual (the marketspace). Banks, for example, provide services to customers at physical branches in the marketplace as well as computerised online services. In South Africa we have automatic teller machines in the marketspace and physical bank branches in the marketplace.

The *Harvard Business Review* got it right on the cyber-money when they told businessmen and businesswomen to **"Pay attention to how your company creates value in both the physical world and the virtual world"**. Those companies that understand both these environments can create and extract value efficiently and effectively.

The Web allows a company to profile itself online, advertise products, create value-added services and, ultimately, derive more revenues. The Web is a multi-dimensional, interactive environment which spans the globe. It has no regard for time zones and it is not confined to traditional trading hours.

The Internet is liberating us from geographical boundaries and from the clock. It makes physical presence immaterial – it operates anywhere, anytime. Wired technology is preparing to obliterate the idea that society can organise everything to run according

There is nothing as useless as doing efficiently that which should not be done at all.

Peter F. Drucker

to set schedules – there is every indication that the "9 to 5" work-day will disappear. For some it already has!

Setting up a Web site establishes another outlet for your products and services. Compare a Web site to a shop in a mall. The shop fittings, salespeople, and cash registers all have digital counterparts on the Web.

Shopping on the Web does not (yet) replace shopping in the physical sense, but it does augment the business process. For example, South Africa's leading news magazine, the *Financial Mail*, launched its online edition, FMi, in late 1995. This interactive online publication lets you subscribe to the hard-copy magazine by simply filling in a form on its Web site. And the hard-copy magazine advertises the Web address of its online counterpart. The marketplace influences activities in the marketspace, and the marketspace reflects back to the marketplace.

Place and Space

Service	Place	Space
banking	bank-teller	auto-teller
postal	post office box	e-mail address
telephone	answering machine	voice mailbox
telephone	Yellow Pages	TelCo directory service

The Internet gives you an alternative – another way of, say, ordering a pizza, setting up an appointment, or settling an overdue account. You choose an infrastructure to communicate based on its appropriateness. For example, you could order your lunch using the postal service, but it would be a little crazy (unless you weren't really hungry). You could make appointments driving to companies and doing so face-to-face, but this would waste time and money. We choose the most efficient infrastructure to get the job done. The Internet is simply another way of doing things – an efficient way.

The Internet, however, is still not as widely used as the telephone, and so it is not the infrastructure of choice when it comes to setting up appointments, for example. But as more and more people start to use the Internet, it will grow in popularity and, when it comes to business, become everybody's first choice in day-to-day communications. As more and more companies set up shop on the Web, the Internet will also become people's first choice when searching and shopping for information, products and services.

The Internet is convenient and efficient. Just think about all the queues we have to endure in the physical world. Nobody enjoys being put on hold indefinitely when they phone an organisation, like a bank, for example. Postal delays are considered just one of those inconvenient things that we just have to live with. The same with traffic jams. But there is another way. The Internet offers an alternative way to communicate and do business. When browsing the products or services offered by an online Web site, you are not subjected to the problems of lunch breaks and understaffing. When you phone your bank to query an account all that happens is somebody taps into a computer and reads the information back to you – why not do it yourself? We should concentrate on looking after the system and improving the system, rather than being the system.

Web of wealth

Establishing a presence on the Web means reaching more people, and that means bigger profit margins. Information is seen as a supporting element in the traditional value chain. A Web site can serve an online community across the globe and add value to any organisation by making information available to a greater and greater audience. This information can represent interactive, value-added services that will save us time, and put us first. Airlines, for example, can sell tickets in both a "place" and a "space".

Federal Express is probably the most inspiring case study to emerge in popular press in this spatial paradigm shift. In the United States, FedEx launched a Web site which allows customers to track a package in transit by connecting to their Web server and entering an airbill number. You can even see where the package is in transit, who signed for it, and so on. This service is provided free, and has created added value for their customers, thus increasing loyalty in a fiercely competitive market. What is even more interesting is how much publicity the company has generated from their Internet initiative. This innovative technical investment gained them some serious market exposure.

The virtual world is redefining economies of scale as digital information can be reused infinitely. The United States Postal Service, for example, could never afford to build a post office in every American's home. Federal Express, however, has done exactly that in the marketspace by allowing individuals with access to the Internet to track packages through the company's presence on the Web. The new economies of scale presented by the Web make it possible for FedEx to provide storefronts to each and every customer, whether one or millions of users request the service at any given time.

The Internet is a vehicle for your business to market itself and to augment your current business practice i.e. to sell more products and services. The Web allows your company to offer new functionality to your target audience in the form of interactive services, consumer hot-lines, product catalogues, shareholder services, and so on.

At this stage in our history it is very sexy to be techno-savvy, and to be setting up shop on the Web. But for Mike Multimedia, consumer at large, there is still no immediate need to get online, other than to discuss this new found sexiness. In fact, many users, after surfing the Web for a few hours, want to get off. But the next couple of years will change that as the world's banks, retailers, travel agents, hotels, newspapers, etc., all scramble to launch online services. Before you know it everyone will want to get online. Because time is money, the Web is proving to be a very efficient shopping experience. Delta Airlines in the USA, for example, are incentivising people to purchase tickets online, and have said that if someone buys an airline ticket over the counter they will pay a surcharge. Every sector of industry is beginning to address the virtual marketplace and realising that the profits are as physical as gold nuggets. From virtual workhorses that have only one purpose: to serve.

There are no free virtual lunches

So, where is all this information everyone is talking about? Many people often ask intriguing questions like, "Why is the *Sunday Times* available online? Is the newspaper company moving from physical to virtual publications? Are they going to phase out their hard-copy paper editions?" We have our own twisted romantic reasoning why we feel the paper version of the *Sunday Times*, for example, will not be replaced by an online counterpart. The first reason is that it is not so cozy to get onto the toilet with a laptop. The second reason: you can't swat a fly with a laptop. Seriously, paper has been around for a long time. We don't think a mere digital revolution is going to change the world that fast.

Before we begin to discuss online information sources, let's put the latest information highway, the Internet, into perspective. The Net is another communications infrastructure. It is an alternative to the telephone, the fax, the postal system and the roads. The value of the Internet lies in the organisations that make use of this infrastructure. The same goes for the telephone and so on. But many people describe the Internet as an information resource. This is not the case. *Time* magazine, for example, is an information resource. The Internet allows you to read *Time* online (www.time.com). Simple as that. If the Internet was a database or a library then so too is the local TelCo and the Post Office. The telephone company simply connects people and organisations to the telephone network. They do not provide the content on this infrastructure. **No one can blame them for a bad conversation. Please stop hating the Internet if you can't find what you are looking for.**

Information-based businesses are the most conducive to online service provision. Media, finance, entertainment, education and other information intensive industries fall into this category. This is why Time Warner, for example, have embraced the Net and this is why the online world has become much more beneficial. Companies like Time Warner have given the Net value. Their efforts on the Web are cutting edge, and the utility derived from their initiative is incredibly powerful and efficient.

But the question still remains: are companies like Time

Warner changing their distribution model?

The only thing that is changing in our opinion is that these type of companies will grow and become more powerful. The Web allows an information publisher to add a tremendous amount of value to its core products. This value adding leads to growth and that means an increase in revenues.

A new breed of online services is being born with all this change. Interactive, real-time gems that will allow us to search, order, query and generally do things that were never practical in the physical world of paper and filing cabinets. Shelf space is dying. Disk space is making a major entrance. As we mentioned before, one cannot phone up the newspaper company and ask them to search for all the issues that dealt with the topic of, say, the Internet in the past 5 years, for example. They simply could not provide this service at a price that you would be prepared to pay. The human resources alone would cost too much. Who is going to run around printing out back issues? Who will pay for these to be couriered across town, or across the planet for that matter? Hey, did someone say "get digital"?

Computers have always been good at storing and retrieving information. The Net allows a company to make information available that was previously simply too expensive to deliver in the physical world. Time Warner, for example, offers services that allow one to search for articles from back issues on its Web site. This is a valuable service and the company will ultimately (in the near future we imagine) derive a new revenue stream from this online initiative.

The search is on

The traditional media, stockbroking, insurance, banking, leisure and entertainment firms of the world are all scrambling to launch online worlds on the Net. Exciting Web sites have been established, for example, by Disney (www.disney.com), Hilton Hotels (www.hilton.com), Federal Express (www.fedex.com), Microsoft (www.microsoft.com), Playboy (www.playboy.com), I-Net Bridge (www.inet.co.za), Nedbank (www.nedbank.co.za), First National Bank (www.fnb.co.za,), Sanlam (www.sanlam.co.za), Time Warner (www.time.com), CNN (www.cnn.com), and many more. But there is also a new generation of online services that has surfaced. Not from blue-chips but from entrepreneurs who saw a gap in the marketspace, and the result: the search engine and searchable directory. Many people are lost in cyberspace looking for their favourite blue-chip organisation's online offering. So they turn to a search engine to point them in the right direction. Just like the telephone system has the "Yellow Pages", so the Web has Yahoo! (www.yahoo.com), Lycos (www.lycos.com), Alta Vista (www.altavista.com) and various other search engines and directories. South Africa has a search engine Ananzi (www.ananzi.co.za) that is dedicated to this part of the globe.

In review, the Web is that part of the Net that is dedicated to the publishing of information and for the provision of interactive, online services. Companies use the Web to add value to their physical offerings and to provide a new generation of services that are fast, cost-effective and multimedia enriched. Without the world's blue-chip organisations setting up shop on the Web, the Net would be a highway with no off-ramps, and we would be driving, er, surfing, aimlessly looking for a way out. We have never heard anyone say, "Stop the virtual world, I want to get off." Well, not these days at least. To all the corporations of planet Earth: well done! Your virtual shops are finally filling in the missing pieces and cyberspace is starting to look a lot more promising.

"Shop until you drop" is being usurped by "surf until you search". Search engines allow you to find what you are looking for fast. Every time a company launches a Web site, the idea is that they should register their virtual shop with the leading search engines. This way you will be able to find things far more easily online.

We vend therefore we are

We are a world of consumers. Behind these shoppers (or in front of them for that matter) is a world of shops. But these physical markets built with bricks and cement are being usurped fast by a virtual world of online shops or Web sites.

The World Wide Web is the place to set up shop, literally. Your market is global, your products are accessible, your message is interactive, and the only limit is your imagination. But what is a world of shops, offline or online, without cash registers? Without a mechanism for payment we would be a world of window shoppers with no economic growth. Enter the SET (Secure Electronic Transaction) standard, developed by VISA and MasterCard – an initiative to establish secure, online, real-time credit card transaction processing via the Web.

Real-time (while you wait) transaction processing via the Web changes everything. The world is moving from surfing and browsing to shopping and spending. Sure, many people surf the malls of this Earth looking and contemplating. But we all spend now and again. Collectively, we spend a lot. The world's economy is growing, and the online world will make it grow even more. The PC transformed this planet – we used to go to picnics, play frisbee and we used to hang out in the park – technology led to the skyscraper, the office park and the shopping mall. And then we became "born to shop". The key word here is "shop". One could have described the virtual community on the Net as a nation "born to surf". But surfing is not where it's at. Doing business is. With new initiatives, like SET for example, the vendors of this planet have just been given the green light to start selling much, much more.

By using SET technologies, banks will enable the world's vendors to accept payments online, in real-time. Vending is the most natural thing we do. Everybody is trying to sell something. With innovations like SET the Web is now officially open for business. Soon you will be able to buy an airline ticket, check into a hotel, rent a car, and order a Christmas pudding over the Web. In real-time. No more queues, no more muggings, and no more congested parking lots and shopping malls. The virtual world is safe, stable and super-fast. It is there, forever waiting, with the patience of eons, for you to spend, spend and spend some more. This is life, offline or online.

Real-time transaction processing is so fundamental. When you shop at Amazon.com, for example, you enter your credit card details and then, after they have processed your financial information, they mail you back about a day later confirming your order. This may be okay for books. But what about a pizza? Or how about an airline ticket that you may need for later on that same day? When we shop we like to do so in real-time. We are a world short on time. We are a world filled with instant gratification junkies. We need service, and we need it now. Real-time processing is not only desirable, it is a necessity for most transactions. Ordering food is the most obvious example. Nobody can wait a day to have their credit card details verified if they are hungry. The same goes for insurance policies, stocks and bonds, hotel reservations, airline tickets and so on.

Tickets themselves are already changing. Just think about it: each printer connected to a PC could be a ticket dispenser. You could be e-mailed an airline ticket, for example, instead of having to collect it from a travel agent. When you arrive at the airport they could check that the number on the ticket is valid and that you are the correct person (by checking your ID). This is already happening right now in the United States. The imagination can run wild here.

Perhaps it is the word "browser" that needs attention. We imagine that in the future this word will be replaced by "shopper". If Netscape and Microsoft would rebrand their Web packages as "shoppers" instead of "browsers" we think that the business world would have more confidence in the online idea of service provision. And this would create more momentum. Imagine if the local mall was called a browsing centre, as opposed to a shopping centre. Surely this would not inspire entrepreneurs to set up shop if all people did was browse? Yes, the online world still has too many people browsing. But with all the new innovations coming to PCs near you, soon they will be shopping.

From retailing to e-tailing

Let's take a brief look at the concept of shopping. When you go into a supermarket, for example, there are typically aisles and aisles of things. Your job is to cruise along these aisles, browsing at different things, picking things out, putting them in your shopping basket and, ultimately, paying for these goods and going home. The aisles of the shop are randomly accessible. There is no set path for our adventures in this physical world. You can choose to go wherever your heart desires. That is why they move things around in the supermarket. One month the peas are in this aisle, the next month, they are way over there. These vendors want us to explore their shops, so that we see more things, and hence buy more. The same goes for the online world. A Web site is randomly accessible. You can navigate through an online world by clicking your mouse on whatever you want. Whatever catches your eye typically influences where you go in the virtual world. That is why maintaining your shop, both offline and online, is so important. People need change. They need to see new things. They need to see new shop window displays. It makes them come back, again and again. Yes, it should be a site for sore eyes.

One of the most intriguing things on the Net is this notion of free information. The world has not changed that much. Nothing is free in this world. When you go shopping in a physical supermarket you can browse and fill up your shopping basket and go home at the end of the day. There is no law against that. Sure, you may drive the shop-keepers a little mad, but there is no law against window shopping. Just to make things even more intriguing, often they let you try things for free when you go shopping. Supermarkets often allow their visitors to sample foods and appliances. But you can't put a salami in your pocket and just walk out the door – ok ok, if you are a male you probably could, because no one would ever stop you and say "Hey, is that a salami in your pocket?" The same goes for the online world. Netizens are often allowed to sample things on Web sites for free: from financial news, to software, to entertainment, to whatever. This is what marketing is all about.

Just like in the supermarket, online consumers can browse all they like. They can even fill up a virtual shopping basket and they can do this all day and night without any charges. It's only when you actually decide to take something home (i.e. to buy something) that you have to pay. Online retailing is not changing life – it is only changing the way we live – not to mention shop. Just like in the supermarket, you can cruise the aisles of cyberspace as long as you want, sampling whatever is being given away, and only spending what and when you want to.

Being first to market is still as important as ever. The Internet has allowed many new age companies to grab valuable market share away from traditional vendors. Amazon.com is one such company that has embraced the opportunities represented by the Web by rapidly launching a virtual bookshop and establishing a powerful, global brand that has taken mind-share of people who traditionally would go to physical bookstores like Barnes and Noble. Amazon.com has built an extensive customer database in a short time by moving fast and by being first to market. The client base they have built up is pretty comfortable with the service. It would take something of significant value to get these customers to swap to an alternative online book seller.

We use the Amazon.com service often. It is reliable and convenient. We log into their Web site using a user-name and password. The hassles of registering with an alternative online service would have to be justified by something seriously compelling. By being first to market, Amazon.com has grabbed some valuable mind-share that was once the property of physical book-stores. There is much to think about here.

Web sites are slowly but surely gaining ground on physical shops. Online shopping is secure, efficient and convenient. As real-time credit card processing enters into the equation the virtual boom is only going to gain momentum. Yes, disk space is usurping shelf space. The world of physical shops is looking less exciting as the virtual world of online Web sites steals the spotlight. You could even go so far as to say that we are physically doomed, but virtually booming. Now that is progress.

There is nothing new about shopping but the methods of shopping are changing. The virtual world is redefining economies of scale, as digital information can be reused infinitely. The Net allows a company to make information available that was simply too expensive to deliver in the physical world. Information can represent interactive, value-added services that will save us time and put us first.

[Nine]

Good-bye emptynets

Intranet. Extranet. Emptynet. The list of new buzz-words just goes on and on. An intranet is that part of an organisation's network that is not for public consumption. In short an intranet is charac- terised by a Web site that has a closed user group. It represents a combination of content, company data and interactivity. Today's intranets are more often than not underdeveloped and unexciting. A typical intranet in a modern corporation is used to publish staff lists and internal telephone directories. Well, these "emptynets" are about to go out of fashion as content, to populate these empty intranets, is just around the corner. It's actually down the super- highway and on your left and right and all over the place. It just needs someone to make it workable.

In this part of the world, new ventures like I-Net Bridge are going to transform our South African emptynets into populated treasure chests of information – functional, informative intranets. It could be simply for a department, or an entire organisation or perhaps a community represented by customers and suppliers (extranets). Web sites are typically for public consumption, where- as intranet sites are for specific audiences (i.e. closed user groups).

When thinking about intranets it is important to consider that the reason many of the corporate initiatives in this arena start with a bang, only to fall flat, is that often the mindset is simply to shift from an old platform to a new one. Take the much talked about online internal telephone directory list, for example. Often this gets shifted to the much hyped new company intranet only to be an HTML version of an old static list. We all need to embrace the new opportunities that Internet technologies bring about. A simple telephone list in our organisation, for example, has been transformed into a productivity tool of note. From searching, to cross referencing, to bulletin boards, to messaging, to digital photographs, and more. A simple thing like an online telephone list can be used to establish an empowering intranet, that saves people time, provides for better communications, and boosts output. Keep this in mind when choosing new technology platforms. When you look beyond the bells and whistles of this exciting multimedia delivery platform, you will see a productivity enhancer that is nothing less than spectacular.

A key word here is leverage. If your company rolls out an intranet, make sure you leverage the capabilities of interactive, distributed system technologies to the maximum. Don't simply shift the challenges of the workplace from one environment to another. **Don't take the limitations that exist in the physical world and put them online. That is what the progress paradox is all about.** And even more importantly, your intranet needs to be maintained and its content needs to be accurate. Quality control is a serious issue.

"Extranets" is one of the latest buzz-word phrases. The definition of an extranet is not entirely clear at this stage. We have heard some people refer to an extranet as that virtual network that is formed by joining two or more intranets. If one closed user group collaborates with another then these two intranets are said to form an extranet. We think the most appropriate definition we have come across is as follows: an extranet is formed when an intranet is opened up, in a secure manner, to allow access to your business partners. In other words, an extranet links your intranet, securely, to the people you do business with (and this may incorporate their intranets as well).

These days just about every organisation on the planet is rolling out an intranet. The word is often misused. An intranet is a Web site. Simple as that. And it is typically used within an organisation to distribute information, share ideas and facilitate collaboration. Does your company have an intranet? If so, what kind of information is made available on your online service? Internal telephone extension directories? The lunch menu? Don't feel alone. This is the basis of many corporate intranets around the globe. Is this really progress? Intranets are going to develop into mission critical environments in the near future. The intranet is going to change from a novelty to a necessity as the world's corporations start to realise that this is an empowerment tool of real significance.

Intelligent intranets

There is so much scope for an intranet beyond the obvious. An intranet seems like the perfect vehicle for moving to a paperless office. But this is just the beginning. We have seen intranets that allow for conferencing, operations tracking, product catalogue distribution, inventory updates, bulletin boards, and much much more. And now, content. Ah, at last. An intranet can be customised to deliver financial news, market trends, weather reports, sports updates, entertainment and whatever information an organisation needs. I-Net Bridge (an online content provider) is one such company that will help the world populate their intranets with South African content, delivered in real-time. Information that is pertinent, credible and cost-effective.

An intranet can serve to empower people at all levels of an organisation. From improved communications to better decision making, to the sharing of ideas and collaboration. An intranet should inform, educate and guide people in the company. The more informed people are the better the decisions that they will make. An intranet can be a key component in any corporate's competitive strategy for the future. Product information and pricing, for example, is key to any sales team in a company. An intranet can be used to publish up-to-date information and it can be used to track inventory and process orders. There is no limit to what is possible here.

Intranets need to be constructed and they need to be maintained. Technically you start by installing a Web server on your computer network. You then need to create meaningful Web pages for your intranet site. So, you will require HTML authors, graphic artists, software engineers, database programmers, systems architects, and so on. But the part that is not obvious pertains to content. Yes, you will need another group of people that will continually update your intranet with worthwhile information. Data about certain consumer trends, market analysis, stock market information, news on mergers and acquisitions, government dispatches, weather reports, entertainment, and more.

So, how do all the parts fit together?

Well, one group of people typically look after the Web server software and the computer hardware itself (that's us – we call them IT people). Another group of people construct Web pages and design graphics etc. (that's also us – we call these people HTML authors, with the ultimate person being responsible, the Webmaster). And yet another group of people specifies the systems architecture and designs hooks into databases and integrates into back-end systems so that your company's data can be stored, manipulated and retrieved via a Web browser. Then, the missing link in moving from an emptynet to an information-rich intranet are people like I-Net Bridge who will deliver a real-time feed of trusted content that can be tailored to your organisation's specific needs.

It is most likely that the same team of people that maintains your public Web site will also look after your intranet Web site within your organisation. The two sites will have different focuses though; the public Web site being sales, marketing and support orientated (customer driven), while the intranet Web site is oriented around operations, strategy, human resources and product information (internally driven).

An intranet is an ongoing initiative. It needs executive buy-in, and it needs to be considered as an ongoing project with a clear owner. Someone needs to drive an intranet within an organisation. We say this because more often than not an intranet initiative has been left to the IT people within an organisation, and hence where the idea of an emptynet arises. The IT people probably did a good job of laying the foundation, but they did not consider how to empower the sales team, or the support staff, or the financial folk, and so on. Content is not top of mind for IT people.

Information that is badly communicated is in fact noise. This is what we face in the world today. We suffer from information overload. Legitimate content providers will help us overcome this dilemma by providing customised information feeds that will serve to empower us to make better decisions, entertain, and simply enlighten us in our specific fields of expertise. Intranets will become an important empowerment tool in any growing organisation. What is truly wonderful is that it will not cost a fortune.

By leveraging your existing computer infrastructure (your LAN and your PCs) you will not have to spend money on proprietary terminals. By utilising Internet technologies, your company can take advantage of a truly open, systemic approach towards communications and the result is a cost-effective vehicle for information dissemination and publication. The legacy proprietary systems that exist in the world today will be usurped by this new scaleable, open platform that allows for a multimedia tour de force. So, watch that screen of yours – there are exciting advancements coming soon to an intranet near you.

From here to eternity and e-commerce

An intranet can be interactive, featuring complex search mechanisms, or it can simply be used to publish text. An intranet can be rich in media, allowing for the delivery of an auditory statement or a video clip. The only limit here is the imagination. Using a standard Web browser (Microsoft Internet Explorer or Netscape Navigator) to view an intranet is key here, and if you haven't yet surfed the Web then get out your wax and secure your footing, because what you see in the public domain is just the beginning. It is what you cannot see that we are talking about here.

Before you know it, you too will be accessing an intranet somewhere to review balance sheets, strategic plans, order forms, contracts, staff lists, company organograms, pension programmes, product news, bulletin boards and much, much more.

A functional intranet or extranet is going to be the key foundation for any successful electronic commerce initiative. Business-to-business e-commerce as well as business to consumer e-commerce is going to rely heavily on content management, knowledge management and application development. Furthermore, a functional intranet initiative will often require integration into back-end legacy systems. This is a real challenge and a significant opportunity for IT suppliers and ISPs. Many companies that use dumb terminals (in a mainframe environment for example) to capture and retrieve information are going to ultimately replace these stone-age machines with Web-based interfaces. These new age terminals will connect to an intranet that can communicate to the back-end legacy system. This approach is open, scaleable and cost-effective.

Web-based information terminals are going to change the way business is done. From the way we book airline tickets, reserve hotel rooms, transfer money between bank accounts, book theatre seats, order pharmaceuticals, to the way we write exams and get educated. Intranets are going to make information storage, retrieval and manipulation far more convenient and efficient. They will transform transaction processing on a global level. A company could, for example, have an intranet site in one country, with data processing terminals in the form of Web interfacing software in other countries very far away.

Punt on portals

A portal is a virtual community. It is a place and space where eyeballs converge. Web sites that have a critical mass of repeat users represent a portal. A portal is the space to sell adverts, mine data, and add value to the virtual world. Think of a portal as the billboard on the side of the road by the airport – when you fly, you buy. Portals are about owning eyeballs. It is eyeballs that browse, and ultimately, shop for goods and services. Currently portals are very topical and many companies are making claims in this regard. The definition of portals is not clearly understood at this point (as any company with a busy Web server is claiming that it's a portal), but their significance in the future sure is.

A successful portal needs to address the following: content, interface design (it needs to be user friendly), interactivity (member created content and logical navigability are highly compelling), and it needs to be highly visible (a successful portal generally requires serious marketing). Entrepreneurs are trying to strike deals all over the place, claiming that their Web site is the next big portal. Portals typically need to be credible and reliable, and marketing is a key issue in this regard. Building and establishing a successful portal typically will require a lot of resources. Companies that have established brands in the physical world, especially in the media sector, can leverage these brands online. CNN, *Time*, *Newsweek*, *Fortune*, Disney, etc. all represent established brands offline. These companies are credible and admired. They are simply leading their established audiences to the online world.

A portal pulls people together online. It represents a virtual community that shares common interests. CNN is a portal. So are Time Warner, Yahoo!, Lycos, Playboy, Netscape, Quicken, and any other site that enjoys a lot of "visits". Hits or visits to a Web site define the value of digital real estate on the Net. Portals enjoy big audiences that come back again and again.

AOL is another portal. The size of the AOL online community is overwhelming. AOL had over 14 million subscribers at the end of 1998. That is 14 million people who log into the AOL environment. That is 14 million people who represent huge buying power. That is 14 million people and growing by the second. In fact, AOL is signing on a new user every few seconds.

An intranet is another form of a portal. It is a private portal. Imagine the reach that an intranet belonging to General Electric or Boeing or Disney can have. Think of any big corporation that makes use of an intranet. Private portals represent closed online communities. We have discussed the significance of content with respect to enriching an intranet. But what about the significance of that closed community? Surely this represents an opportunity for companies selling goods and services to brand themselves right into the foundation of these private portals?

Amazon.com or CDnow, for example, could strike deals with a company to incorporate their offerings into that company's private portal i.e. their intranet. Just think about this for a minute. Your company could build an intranet, get content from a provider like I-Net Bridge, and have value-added service agreements from the likes of Amazon.com and CDnow. Perhaps all the members of your organisation will get a special discount if they order books off your intranet via these vendors. Perhaps the combined buying power of your aggregated users will get you even better deals. The possibilities are endless. From book clubs, to reviews, to recommendations, to vertical communities. A private portal represents opportunity upon opportunity. Again, the only limit is the imagination.

The benefits to your organisation could be incredible. An intranet can be used to create greater loyalty amongst your staff by building a stronger sense of community and by looking after their day-to-day needs more effectively. Productivity levels can increase as a result of faster decision making due to greater information availability. Just think about the possibility of tying in a supermarket to your company's intranet. If someone in your organisation needs to go out and buy stuff for the house then that too could be done online. The time that can be saved is overwhelming. And because all purchases made via your company's intranet with outside vendors will go through a central point, the accounting benefits and economies of scale that could be realised are tremendous. A salary sacrifice scheme could be introduced for your staff to help them obtain more tax breaks, for example.

The list of vendors that could collaborate with you on your company's intranet is endless. And for these vendors what could be more exciting? They get to reach a canned audience made of solid income earners.

Furthermore, your company could choose to underwrite all purchases made and obtain better pricing as a consequence for all your staff. Vendors could be guaranteed payment and they would certainly benefit from having a central delivery point. All purchases made could be delivered to the front desk and this consolidation would lead to even more saving and hence more benefits for all concerned. Vendors could also negotiate to be the exclusive providers to your company, with respect to their products and services, with even better pricing for all your staff. Amazon.com, for example, may sign an agreement to be the exclusive book seller to an organisation, with a central delivery point, guaranteed payment, and better pricing for all the members of that online community.

Yes, there is no doubt, the private portal is a significant realisation – a company's intranet is the portal of the future.

The intranet is going to change from a novelty to a necessity as the world starts to realise this is an empowerment tool of real significance. An intranet will be a key component in your company's competitive strategy for the future. A well maintained intranet saves people time, provides for better communications, and boosts output.

The most
powerful network
is *not* the *Internet* – it is the
human network.

David Frankel

Logic will get
you from
A to B.
Imagination will
take you
everywhere.

Author Unknown

You see things that are
and say,

"Why?"

But I dream things that
never were and say,

"Why not?"

Robert F. Kennedy

In matters of style,
swim with the current;
in matters of principle,
stand like a rock.

Thomas Jefferson

There are 24 hours in the day, and then there's the night.

Barry Hore

Luck favours the persistent.

James Collins and Jerry Porras

When I was a boy of fourteen, my father was so ignorant. I could hardly stand to have the old man around. But when I got to be twenty-one, I was astonished at how much he had learned in seven years.

Mark Twain

[Ten]

World Wide Wisdom

Electronic commerce over the Web is going to revolutionise the way we work, shop, live and play. The Internet and the rapid emergence of associated online trends is an intriguing phenomenon. With each step forward in Internet communications, technology moves another step forward. And one step back. This is the progress paradox in a nutshell. Every time someone invents a more efficient way to communicate online, people around the world use this to their advantage, and work more, and invent more. So much more gets developed because of all this continuous development.

This sounds a little strange, we know. But just think about this for a minute. While we were putting this book together, we upgraded PCs, installed a new operating system, and loaded up the latest word processor software, only to discover that our editors were using older versions that were not compatible with our ones. We had to go backwards quite often before we could go forwards. Now that's progress.

Personalisation (often referred to as one-to-one marketing) is one of the most exciting trends on the Web today. Have you ever been to a Web site where they welcome you back, and where they have a history of your online shopping activity?

Amazon.com, the famous virtual bookstore that hails itself as "Earth's biggest bookstore", is one example of personalisation at work. When you go back to their Web site (assuming you have already bought something there before) they will have all your details, your shopping history, your list of gift recipients and what you have sent them (if you have ever needed to send someone a present then this is a great way to go), and so on. Then comes the amazing stuff. Suggested titles, book reviews, related material, and more. Yes, they serve you personalised information based on your online history with them.

For example, if we order a book on networking and a book on electronic transaction processing, then they may present us with a list of books that deal with electronic commerce. The possibilities are endless. Virtual vertical communities (i.e. online communities of doctors, lawyers, bankers, analysts, scientists, journalists, sports fans, students, and so on) are going to spring up all over the globe with these types of initiatives. Want to join a discussion group on SET technologies? Then look no further. Just point and click.

Working Web

As Web sites evolve from non-commercial applications through simple transactions to service-based e-commerce, the level of sophistication and complexity of applications will increase accordingly. Still in the early stages of development, service-based Web e-commerce requires rich content applications characterised by user-focused personalisation, native interactivity, exploratory navigation, and continuous growth. These characteristics, in turn, require architectural structures that separate content and development, and which enable adaptive navigation. A successful Web e-commerce application must be based on a system that meets all of these architectural requirements.

The characteristics of content applications demand that the application development (and software delivery environment) meet four specific criteria: the separation of information (content) and the way it's presented on the Web, the dynamic construction of Web pages of information, information management, and adaptive navigation support (i.e. navigation that is able to adapt to a user's needs).

Existing system architectures either cannot meet these requirements, or cannot meet them efficiently and cost-effectively. A content-component approach coupled with a rich application-serving environment, however, eliminates the problems inherent in existing architectures – it is an appropriate methodology for developing and deploying content applications for service-based Web e-commerce.

Web applications have expanded rapidly through several stages: brochure sites pushing primarily text-based information with simple graphics; sites for e-commerce in digital goods such as electronic publishing and software downloads; storefront sites targeting markets for hard goods such as PCs, CDs and books; service-based sites which offer customers much more than simple transactional commerce.

The early brochure sites served primarily as sources of information and did not have capabilities for either conducting e-commerce or for fulfilling specific business objectives. These sites were rapidly supplanted by the first commercial sites, which dealt primarily in digital goods. These sites, in turn, gave way to virtual storefronts where users could buy hard goods over the Internet.

The early storefront sites focused on hard goods with low consideration buying patterns (in which customers generally entered transactions already having decided what to buy). The most obvious examples were commodity items such as books, CDs and PCs. These sites gave rise to the technical challenges of managing transactions and commerce over the Web, which in turn launched an entire industry of transaction-centric application environments.

Today, Web sites are in the process of evolving beyond selling commodity goods and serving niche markets. Rather than simply engaging users in commercial transactions, they are broadening their capabilities to attract and retain users as well. This requires providing a level of value and service which was, until now, not a necessary component of Web commerce.

Attracting new customers to a Web site requires a content base that will appeal to a potential customer and keep him or her engaged with rich multimedia and interactive experiences. Retaining a customer after engagement requires personalising the content to stimulate continued interest and use over time.

Help wanted

Consider an example of an electronic helpdesk designed to provide users with online support for products they have purchased. The customer support Web site is a classic content application that contains many different elements such as bulletin boards, chat rooms, and knowledge bases which users can explore to find answers to their questions. The business objectives driving such an application are threefold:

- Reduce support costs by replacing as many phone calls as possible with Web site visits.
- Build brand reputation by ensuring customers can use the product successfully.
- Drive additional revenue by exposing customers to other products and product uses.

Meeting these business objectives raises several important challenges: navigation, content segmentation, interactivity, and the stimulation of online sales.

To meet its business objectives, the customer support application requires a deep knowledge base. This immediately presents a fundamental challenge: how will customers efficiently find the information they need? If finding the information they need is difficult, they will reach for the phone instead. The site must have a powerful and intuitive navigation system that allows customers to find information quickly and efficiently.

A search engine alone cannot solve this problem. In most cases a customer entering a support application has only the vaguest idea of what to look for. Furthermore, the larger the knowledge base, the more difficult it is to formulate an effective search-engine query; most queries on broad topics will return hundreds of results.

An exploratory navigation approach can overcome the limitations of the search-engine paradigm. For example, rather than perform a search for a particular source of information, a customer can enter a keyword and receive customised navigation screens with which to refine their search. Refining (i.e. iterating) through this procedure manually enables the customer to perform a self-directed search with the *assistance* of the application, not at the *mercy* of the application.

With the large knowledge base that characterises the customer support application, a key function is the ability to show different views to different customers. For example, a company might display different screens to different customers depending on which products they own. This could mean providing each customer with a customised navigation bar for top-level topics about their products. As another example, there might be a "premium" area of the site that shows selected customers restricted information. In this case, some content might be available initially in the premium area only, and later made available to all site visitors. Such a situation would require the ability not only to segment content, but also to combine it in different ways as needed.

To meet its business objectives of reducing support costs and building brand reputation, the customer support application should also include a means of allowing customers to contribute their own content to the knowledge base and thus build a community of users over time. A message bulletin-board system within such an application allows customers to answer each other's questions by interacting with each other directly, thus eliminating support costs for the company. As customers provide most of the content, the bulletin-board system requires the site to support high levels of interactivity.

Promotional elements within customer support applications can help meet the objective of driving additional sales revenue. Like the problem-resolution section of such a site, this section requires a rich and dynamic navigation structure, although for an entirely different reason. Whereas in the problem-solving area the value lies in how quickly the customer can finish using the application, in the promotional area the value is measured by how long the customer remains engaged. For this reason, tedious navigation systems and static content, which discourage lengthy customer exploration, must be avoided.

A Web way

Content applications must shape and present information in a way that is relevant to users in order to keep their attention. For example, consider the "installation help" feature of a site that provides customer support for software products. Customer requirements will vary depending on hardware platform, system configuration, and many other variables. Only by delivering extremely specific, customised instructions will the application achieve its business objective of reducing telephone support costs.

Content applications are inherently exploratory: users take unknown paths, perform unpredictable actions and work towards non-specific goals. A user's engagement with the site ends not when any specific action has been completed, but when the user feels satisfied. Navigation tools and personalisation services must therefore take into account the nebulous nature of the user's experience.

Many Web applications are interactive only in trivial ways: filling in a field on a search form, selecting a few preferences, and so forth. But in a content application, users are often also authors who contribute directly to the application as the customer support example illustrates. As the application does not distinguish between users and authors, interactivity can be said to be native to the application. Therefore, support for interactivity must also be native in the application development and run-time environment (i.e. when the application software is actually running and the system is in fact live).

If a content application is successful, the size of its content base will inevitably grow. Indeed, success may actually be measured by the growth of the content base. The customer support application is a good example of the building of a knowledge base from customer experiences. Therefore growth is an intrinsic element of content-driven applications.

The previously described characteristics of content applications are related to four specific architectural requirements. First, content must be separated from presentation in order to allow users without technical expertise to provide content. Second, the page-assembly mechanism must be dynamic so that content can be incorporated, combined and recombined as needed. Third, content management and delivery must be integrated so that changing content can be efficiently managed during run time. Finally the navigation system must be designed to adapt to different types of users.

Content applications are inherently interactive and regularly changing. The people supplying content to the application are as likely to be visitors to the site as they are to be developers or internal content contributors. It is simply not practical to require the entire community of users to know anything about the layout rules of the application or the mechanics of how the application is updated. This is why content and presentation must be separate components of the system architecture so users can supply content without regard for how it will be displayed or used.

The content-driven site must have the capability of dynamically organising content which is constantly changing and, at the same time, assemble it for users who expect their own customised views of the application. Yet, static information architectures can not scale to serve the exploratory needs of the end-users as the content base continues to grow.

This requires the application to have the ability to dynamically organise and assemble the appropriate content for the end-users based on all available data, which might constantly change. Thus, content applications must be capable of dynamic assembly of individual content components, whereby the application can reorganise itself to present varying views of information to different users or even to the same user at different times.

This is fundamental to building helpful, adaptive navigation systems and effective information architectures. The practical implementation of dynamic assembly also requires self-aware content: the application must have a robust, extensible meta data (information about information) system that allows the application to know something about the content contained within it and how to recombine that content in new ways.

Meta data puts information into context i.e. meta data describes the context of the information. The meta data about "DO YOU LOVE IT IN THE MORNINGS?" is that it is a title. Additional examples would pertain to the names of the authors, the ISBN book number, and so on. Meta data serves to identify both the origin and the nature of any form of content. A major problem on the Web today is that there is a fortune of information online but much of it is out of context; and information that is out of context is meaningless. The progress paradox is evident here: we have more information in the world but not enough knowledge.

Content applications blur the distinction between development and delivery. For example, visitor-supplied content must be kept together and may need a workflow for review, approval and launch into the live environment. In a customer support application, customers must be able to log service calls (and in the process get issued with a "trouble ticket" or service number for tracking purposes so that the customer can easily follow this up at any stage), and incidents must be routed to customer support personnel while, at the same time, the service call incident appears as an open item to visitors of the site.

Content management must occur not only during development of a Web site, but also during its entire life-time. For example, project management and workflow tracking tools must work in the development phase as well as the entire system's life-span.

Adaptive navigation provides users with a personalised implementation structure to assist them in accomplishing their goals. Executed successfully, it reduces user frustration in complex sites and increases the probability and frequency of return visits. One must keep in mind, however, that the user goals which adaptive navigation and personalisation are meant to address may be ill defined and nebulous, or even completely unknown. For this reason, simple rules-based personalisation paradigms are of little use in content-driven sites.

For example, if a customer goes to a Web site with the specific goal of purchasing a first-class airline ticket, it stands to reason that this customer might also be interested in five star hotels or luxury rental cars. The traditional rules-based paradigm works fine in this instance. But in a content application, users not only tend to pursue unknown goals, they also take unknown paths to get there. Therefore, the rules-based paradigm can tend to offer less value in suggesting navigational strategies. What is required instead is a more interactive and self-learning or iterative approach to personalisation, one that focuses on building navigation systems that can adapt to the dynamic nature of the customer's site experience. In such an approach the application can be designed essentially to personalise itself, by using dynamic assembly techniques, allowing the user to build up his or her own unique context and views of information. Forrester Research's report, 'Personalise or Perish' (May, 1997), calls this concept "dynamic customisation."

Unified Messaging

Just when we thought we had seen it all – and heard it all – we experienced a mind-blowing demonstration of Unified Messaging (UM). Our first reaction was: Wow! You can listen to e-mail over the phone (and reply), have yourself paged when new messages arrive, retrieve faxes over the Net, listen to your voice mail via the Web, and the visitors (to these Web sites) just keep on coming.

UM is a messaging revolution that leverages the portability, ease and power of the Internet by taking your e-mail, voice mail, fax and pager and integrating them all into a single Web-based "inbox" that you can access from anywhere on the Internet. If you have access to the Internet then you can retrieve a fax, for example, that has been sent to you via a telephone number in the United States, or anywhere else for that matter.

Have you ever tried to do business in the USA? Have you ever handed out a business card with, for example, a South African telephone or fax number on it? How many people have called you or faxed you from the USA? We thought so. They have never heard of us. Besides being highly efficient and cost-effective, the UM service offerings we have witnessed to date are the answers to all these questions. With this type of technology you can have a telephone number in America that people can call up, for example, and leave you a voice mail message. You can then retrieve your messages over the Web and call them back.

Imagine listening to voice mail, via your computer, that has been left for you in another country. This really is amazing. Yes, we are very excited about the possibilities that these new initiatives represent. There are two kinds of options that we have seen (and heard) on the Web with respect to the audio stream: WAV format and RealAudio. WAV files represent audio clips which one could download from a Web site, in this case, to your computer. It can then be saved and played back on your PC speakers. RealAudio is a newer technology which provides for real-time audio streams to be established online i.e. there are no long waits – you click, you hear. RealAudio is a quantum leap forward as it circumvents the long waiting periods typically associated with file downloads. Both work really well and it is amazing to see how easy this service is to use. It also allows you to retrieve faxes that people send to your new American telephone number. Just think about it: someone sends you a fax via a telephone in the USA, you then fire up your Web browser and go and view that fax right here in South Africa. Ultimately what you have here is a universal inbox that can handle your voice mail, faxes, e-mail, and so on.

We have also seen some touch-tone telephone options which blew us away even more. You can call your new universal inbox from a normal telephone, punch in your password, and listen to your e-mail.

There is no more efficient way to communicate than e-mail. You're probably already dependent on it. But e-mail has one inherent limitation: you need a computer with an Internet connection to retrieve it. Until now, that is.

With the new system a text to voice software engine lets you listen to your e-mail using a normal telephone. You can then reply to a message by talking into the phone. By following some simple menu-driven instructions on a touch tone phone you can retrieve and reply to e-mail from anywhere in the world, without a PC! When you reply, your voice message is digitised and sent as an audio attachment to the recipient's e-mail address. That person then simply listens to your voice on their computer.

Let's have a brief look at how this works. You sign-up with a UM service (check out www.tems.com or www.vpon.com or www.messagepoint.com for some good UM implementations). They issue you with a telephone number and a password. The telephone number forms part of a universal e-mail address. For example, if the number you get is 283-5000, then the e-mail address will be something like 2835000@domainname.com. People can send e-mail to this address, and you can phone this number and listen to your mail messages, and so on.

Supercharge your e-mail with Unified Messaging! Just think of how powerful this technology is: you can be overseas, without a computer, and you can call up your new telephone number and listen to an important message and reply to it. This is reliable, cost-effective and easy to use. You can retrieve any kind of message with whatever kind of communications device you have at your disposal: a PC, a cell-phone or a call-box.

If you are one of those who suffer from e-mail overload then "filters" are another functional option that could really save you time. We imagine that future UM initiatives will allow for intelligent filters that will prioritise your mail queue. So, if you were expecting an e-mail reply from Bill Gates (it could happen) when you called up your UM telephone number, those messages would be first in line. This could really streamline our day-to-day activities.

Voice recognition software has always been a fascinating challenge. One day we imagine that cell-phones will be able to perform quality voice recognition functions. You may be thinking: so what? Well, imagine that once your cell-phone has converted your voice into text that it e-mails off that message to someone on the Net. Yes, you speak into your phone, press a button, and presto, a message appears in someone's mailbox somewhere on the Net. Wow!

Go and check – or hear – it out, and listen to your messages. More and more media streams are converging. We are sure there will be more where this came from.

CTI (Computer Telephony Integration) is one last concept we want to highlight. CTI is about integrating computer systems, namely databases, with call centres. Now, throw in the Web as an intermediary and what you have is a customer support vehicle of global proportions. Imagine having a Web site that says "Fill in your name and number and click the button below and a service representative will call you within a minute." Furthermore, calls can be scheduled. You can book a time when you want someone to call you.

Supply chains are going to be flattened as disintermediation (the removal of intermediaries/middle-men) becomes the order of the day. Supply chain management services are going to diminish in value as the world becomes more end-user oriented. Customer-centric environments are the new norm in the virtual world. The temporal length of the traditional supply chain will shrink as technology streamlines communications flow. Integrated call centres and Web-based e-commerce represent one step closer in this direction.

With all these technological advancements, the real challenge that needs to be emphasised is our ability to move towards an online shopping environment that is seen as an extension of the real world. Ease of use is the key to success here. Virtual shopping needs to be as easy as physical shopping. When we reach that point the difference between online and offline will be history, as Web stores become as ubiquitous as their physical counterparts. And the progress paradox will be there, intriguing us more than ever, as the scope to save time will be even greater, but our ability to enjoy this time will become less.

Virtual shopping needs to be as easy as physical shopping. When we reach that point, the difference between online and offline will be history as Web stores become as ubiquitous as their physical counterparts. Customer-centric environments are the new norm in the virtual world.

[Jack]

Let's get our fax straight!

Put your business online or put your business on the line. Yes, the way things are going, if you don't have a Web-enabled business in the next five years, say, then you won't be doing as well as you could be. In fact, you may not be doing much at all. Electronic commerce over the Internet, specifically business to consumer transactions, is going to change the world, and forever.

The current business methodology for selling goods and services via the Web is based on offline credit card processing. For example, if one buys a T-shirt, book, PC or CD online, then that virtual vendor characteristically processes your credit card details the old fashioned way (by calling the bank). And that explains why these vendors need to e-mail you back with a verification message many hours later, sometimes, a whole day later if you are online from South Africa and browsing a site in, say, the USA.

This may be okay for these kinds of goods, but there are many industries where this is not sufficient for functional e-commerce to take place. Just think about it, if you want to eat then you need to be able to order food right away. Yes, ordering a pizza needs to happen in real-time. No one orders a pizza using the postal service – this is a transaction that has to occur in real-time.

The same goes for insurance, banking, stockbroking, airline reservations, theatre bookings, medical prescriptions, and so on.

Not to mention media companies that are all anxiously looking for new ways to derive revenues online. When people want news they want it right away. Old news is not good news in this day and age. One of the biggest challenges that these companies face is that of providing a real-time payment mechanism for the purchase of services online.

What we need is real-time credit processing. What we need is a way to enable all those vendors out there who don't have online infrastructure. Yes, what about all those sidewalk stores that don't have online network connectivity? Having an online brochure is one thing. But having an interactive, real-time, secure, transaction processing engine is something else altogether. So, how are we going to enable *all* the vendors out there?

The Web is going to be transformed as we witness the roll-out of technologies such as SET (Secure Electronic Transaction). The SET protocol is the great e-commerce enabler. SET initiatives are going to put the *oomph* into electronic commerce. Real-time transaction processing for your favourite credit card is just a mouse click away as online SET-based Web sites get rolled out in the years ahead. Yes, real online shopping is not far away. Global, 24 hours, secure and in real-time. For a world full of shoppers, SET is going to make Prozac look like a decaf latte.

SET enables full secure, end-to-end, Internet credit card transactions. The development of the protocol has been led by VISA and MasterCard. SET version 1.0, which made its entrance in 1997, represents the first true milestone in secure, real-time Internet transactions. SET is an evolving standard, especially in the area of certification logistics and other forms of payment besides credit cards (e-cash, e-cheques, etc.). SET is a four-party protocol involving the customer, the merchant, the acquiring bank, and the Certification Authority (CA). The CA is an independent body that is authorised to issue digital certificates (the ID-cards of the Web). Examples of CA's are Verisign, GTE and SACA (the South African Certification Authority, who were pretty fast off the mark to endorse e-commerce in this land).

We are going to discuss something that will require you to open your mind and think about the following: if you have a Web site, then you will be able to fulfil people's orders in real-time by utilising SET. The large financial institutions have big computer networks and lots of IT resources to automate, say, the real-time processing of the sale of a financial service.

But how does one order a pizza online from Pop's Pizzeria Web site, for example, and then have Pop's get the chefs to do their magic? In short, you can use your credit card via the Web to order something in real-time by utilising SET technologies, but how do the offline counterparts (the actual physical shops) get to process the order? In other words, how will Pop's Pizzeria know if you have ordered something from them via their Web site, be it real-time or not?

The current business to consumer model for Web-based commerce does not exploit the real-time processing introduced by SET. That should explain why services like Amazon.com and CDnow, for example, generally take up to 24 hours to get back to you once you have ordered books or CDs from them. The reason no one worries too much is because books and music that arrive a little late are still usable. But if you are hungry and you want a pizza then you don't want to wait 24 hours to have your credit card details checked and cleared offline (i.e. not in real-time).

So, how does Pop's Pizzeria get to find out that you ordered a pizza from them and that your money has been transferred, i.e., that the funds have gone through to Pop's (while exploiting SET technology on their Web site)?

One could, say, put Pop's online. Yes, that would be one route to take, but would Pop's want to start running routers, PCs and leased lines? Will Pop's Pizzeria have an IT department? If PCs and routers etc. were small and easy to install, and if leased line Internet access cost a couple of bucks then Pop's would be keen. And so would every shop on the planet that does not have IT infrastructure. But unfortunately PCs need attention, routers cost a bit, and leased lines and online Internet access will cost a bit more. So, how does Pop's get to actually make you a pizza once you have placed an order via their Web site? Did someone say we have all the fax? Yes, fax!

Fax is another route. And it is simple, pervasive and

cost-effective. If you went over to Pop's Pizzeria site on the Web, you could enter your credit details, choose something off the menu and the Web site could fax the order to the fax machine that Pop's has been using for years. The fax can even have your name on it and your credit card details so that when you go and collect your goods you can verify that you are who you say you are. If Pop's delivers then it can even fax them your address and the time you want it delivered. This could be a very powerful e-commerce enabler.

You could, for instance, order pizzas for a big function you have that afternoon at the click of a mouse. Pop's gets the fax and the ball is set in motion. Fax is one instrument that can bridge the gap between the "have" and the "have not". If you don't have an Internet link, but you run a small shop, and you want to run a Web site and process orders in real-time utilising SET, then your good old faithful fax machine may be just the thing you need to complete the process.

Yes, surf's up for everyone with this idea in mind. All the vendors of this planet can roll-out Web sites with SET technologies that can process credit card based orders in real-time. With online connectivity they can get orders dispatched as soon as money is in the bank (actually, as soon as the confirmation is in the e-mail). If your company does not have IT infrastructure, then a fax machine is an interesting alternative. A Web site can be developed to incorporate a fax gateway quite easily. And you thought the Web was a high-tech domain!

Many ideas have been presented in this short chapter. Let us summarise what has been discussed: a vendor can build a Web site and have it housed by an ISP; furthermore, any vendor can put up a SET enabled Web site (provided your ISP provides this type of service) to cater for real-time credit card processing online; and finally, any vendor can be notified of a legitimate sale of their goods or services from their Web site by being online or by using a fax machine.

When a fax comes through it means that someone on the Net has been to your company's Web site, filled in their credit card number (and their details etc.), ordered some goods and services, and the fax simply completes the transaction. If the online user did not have funds, say, and their credit card was rejected, then you would not have to receive a fax. The Web site can inform that user right there and then because SET allows for real-time credit card processing. When a fax does come through it means a real sale has been made and you then need to process the order and dispatch the goods or services that have been ordered and paid for. Just think about IT: the more the fax machine works, the more you work. What a wonderful world.

So much functionality can be built into this simple idea. Each day the Web site could send you a fax listing the day's transactions. The ability to audit this type of initiative is incredibly useful and efficient. Each fax can represent an invoice with a unique, sequential invoice number. The possibilities are endless. Furthermore, this idea can be implemented securely and is not prone to abuse or human error.

Once again, we have to look to the past to gain in the future. Don't throw out that trusty old fax machine just yet.

Yes, the progress paradox is here again. Fax certainly is stranger than fiction.

The current business model for consumer transactions on the Web does not exploit real-time processing of financial information. When you buy a book or a CD online, for example, it generally takes up to 24 hours for a vendor to get back to you with an e-mail message confirming (or declining) your purchase. Books and CDs that arrive a little late are still usable. But what if you are hungry and want to order a pizza? You don't want to wait 24 hours to have your credit card details checked and cleared offline. Real-time credit card processing is the next step in Web-based commerce.

[Queen]

From the Dollar Bill
to the Bill Dollar

You have content, you have a Web site, and you also have seen the movie "Field of Dreams". You know that if you build it they will surf, er, buy. So, you have created an online store and people are browsing away like there's no tomorrow. But no one is spending. Well, one reason could be that maybe there is no tomorrow in cyberspace (what time do shops close online?). The other more compelling reason is that online payment mechanisms are still in their infancy.

The world's prognosticators once predicted the end of the Dollar Bill and the birth of the Bill Dollar (Microsoft Money that is), but the cyberbuck stops right here. Real currency will be spent on real goods as the world's banks start to open their doors, or rather, their home pages, to you, the ex-surfer, now new-age shopper. We don't imagine that the virtual bank and its associated e-cash are going to be the norm. Shopping paradigms will change, but the balance of power shouldn't. Banks control the offline world, so why should the online world be any different? Companies like Microsoft are in a great position in terms of getting a slice of the action. Their PC desktop market-share and their diversification into e-commerce puts them ahead of most. But don't expect to throw out your Dollar bills just yet.

If SET (Secure Electronic Transaction) is embraced on the

Your vision
will become clear
only when you can
look into your own
heart.
Who looks outside,
dreams;
who looks inside,
awakes.

Carl Jung

Web then we imagine that the balance of power will remain as is. AOL may charge vendors a lot to be the exclusive provider to their online community (a captive marketspace), but VISA and MasterCard, for example, will still get their money when you make a purchase in the virtual world.

Trust is everything in this world, physically or virtually. The historically trusted brands in the financial services arena will be the foundation of any payment vehicle online. For a company to launch themselves as a new financial agent online is going to be an incredible effort, practically impossible considering the credibility one needs to establish. No, we don't think that the idea of a new virtual bank with some new kind of cyberbuck will make it into the mainstream.

When you go shopping online you consciously make a decision to go to a particular Web site and partake in its offerings. Some Web sites are purely promotional in nature and some offer functional utility, as in the case with the online banking services.

Well, if you were wondering if it's safe to do your banking online then all we have to say to you is, "We live in Johannesburg – we will take our chances online any day of the week – we never heard of anyone getting mugged or hijacked using the Web". The physical world is not as safe as it used to be. The virtual world is a lot more peaceful, with or without encryption. With the right implementation, online transaction processing is secure, reliable, scaleable and efficient.

Game, SET and match

We don't know who will win the match, but a race is definitely on. And the name of the game is money. Using SET mechanisms on the Web, virtual vendors are going to supersede physical shopkeepers as we move from trading places to trading spaces. The SET protocol allows consumers, merchants and financial institutions to safely utilise credit card numbers and other sensitive information over the Internet in real-time. As the saying goes, time definitely is money. Real-time credit card enabled transactions are going to add up to lots and lots of hard currency in the online world.

*It is useless to desire more **time** if you are already wasting what **little** you have.*

James Allen

In the early Internet days (just a few years ago), the vast majority of the online community did not trust this new channel as a mechanism for transaction processing (i.e. online shopping was not the done thing). In short, people have been afraid to use their credit card numbers via the Web. But SET will change all this. The Web merchants of cyberspace have already started to embrace strong encryption techniques for financial transactions and digital signatures. Secure electronic transactions will be a way of life in the next century. It will all be done in real-time. This digital direction will ultimately mean reduced credit card fraud, increased privacy, and more personalised service. As consumers, we will be better off on the Web than on the roads. After all, no one ever gets mugged while surfing the Web.

So, what are we waiting for? The banks. The banks are the key players here. That shouldn't surprise you. The banks hold all the physical keys, so, why wouldn't they hold the virtual keys. In the online world, the banks are the missing link. The banks need to embrace SET-enabled transactions via the Web so that we can all stop browsing and start shopping. After all, we were all born to surf, er, shop. We want to shop online, from the comfort of our own homes (and PCs and modems of course).

The traditional online shopping environment that has been established on the Net over the past couple of years has moved from crude user interfaces to stylish and ergonomically-sound Web-based pages that are interactive and functional. Security has, and always will be, a valid concern and much effort is being spent in the area of cryptography to ensure that all our confidential data is not compromised. We have witnessed the Secure Sockets Layer (SSL) mechanism that was pioneered by Netscape, and this is just the beginning. These days your data is pretty safe when in transit over the Net. With all this, there is still something missing. Time. The time that it takes for a transaction to be authorised via the Web is not currently that exciting. In fact, it is a pain in the butt. When you first sign on to an online store, like CDnow or Amazon.com, you have to wait for them to e-mail you with the results of your purchase: yay or nay. Nothing is more frustrating than getting a message a day later saying, "Sorry, your credit card

The object of work is living, experience, happiness. All that money can do is buy someone else's work in exchange for our own.

Henry Ford

has been declined" or whatever.

In the physical world of shopping malls, our credit card transaction gets processed in real-time (i.e. while we wait – true, sometimes we wait a little too long like during Christmas, but we still get served that day). This is because each vendor or merchant is connected to all the banks, literally, by way of those swipe-card machines. This other virtual network that has been created is an integral part of our lives. Without it we would not be able to whip out our plastic with so much enthusiasm. That is what is needed on the Web, more enthusiasm. Enthusiasm will drive the move from browser to shopper. It is the real-time factor that underpins this enthusiasm. SET technology will allow a Web site (an online virtual shop) to process your credit card information in real-time. You will be able to get a response while you surf, er, wait.

How does this work? Well, just like in the physical world of swipe-card terminals, the Net is about machines all talking to one another, so the transition is quite straightforward. Each online merchant will be connected over the Internet to the banks via a three way communications protocol between the user (that's us, the consumers), the merchant, and the bank representing the credit card company that authorises the payment to go through. The credit card companies in this case will be the online counterparts of the brands of plastic we know so well, and the banks that represent these brands: VISA, MasterCard, AMEX, Diners Club, and so on. Yes, like we said, the browser is in their court. Come on banks. Let's SET this one on its digital path for non-stop, 24 hour, online shopping. It is a win-win. We get to shop more, and you get to make more money per transaction. We all win.

SET is one initiative in the area of online transaction processing. If SET is not the chosen vehicle in years to come then it will be some other industry manufactured standard that will. The point we are making is that regardless of what technical methodologies are used, you can bet that the giants like VISA, MasterCard, AMEX, Diners Club, and the rest, will all be involved. The idea behind virtual banks and virtual currency or e-cash is exciting, but we think that the traditional credit card vendors are going to be the dominant payment force online. Yes, the balance of power stays as is.

I can't understand
why people are frightened
by new ideas.
I'm frightened of
old ones.

John Cage

Aladdin

Open sesame! Aladdin was a joint venture between our organisation and MTN (one of South Africa's largest cell-phone operators) that uses GSM smartcard devices to control charges securely for access to a Web site. Aladdin addresses three fundamental online issues: how to identify – securely – the user driving the Web browser; how to bill the user for small charges (micro-payments); and how to enable existing Web sites to earn revenues.

Cellular telephony involves the use of devices which already use smartcard technology to control who can utilise a cellular phone. In others words, the PIN number that you enter when you turn the device on, tells the SIM card that you are allowed to use the phone. The other exciting feature about the SIM card is the fact that it tells the network who you are so that you can be billed. That is why, if you take your SIM card and use it in someone else's phone, you get billed and not them. Aladdin is essentially a product that has been developed to use the features of both the SIM card and the GSM network.

The following sequence of events occurs when Aladdin is used:

- You begin by pointing your Web browser to an Aladdin-enabled Web site.
- The Aladdin service then challenges you with a page that says, "This site is Aladdin protected – please use your cell-phone to dial the following number – 19xxyyzz)." The xx portion of the number identifies which Aladdin service you are using, the yy number identifies the Web site, and the zz number identifies the specific Web session on the Web site.
- You dial the number you are prompted for. Your SIM card's CLI (Caller Line Identity) is transferred to the Web site via the Aladdin service and the GSM network. (How long does it take? From the time you hit call on the phone – about 3 seconds!)
- The Web site uses the CLI to say, "Hello Joe Soap". You are then either granted or denied access to the site.

Aladdin then manages the state of the Web server by permitting you to partake in the service on offer. The service could be as simple as accessing a research report online or as complex as paying for an airline ticket. You can also use Aladdin to do authentication i.e. to verify that someone is who they say they are without the user having to remember and type passwords and user-names.

With Aladdin you have an innovative way to charge a user for access to online information. Remember that whenever you make a cell-phone call, you get billed by a cellular network – the xx portion of the Aladdin number could reflect the amount you pay i.e. $1 if you dial 1901, $2 if you dial 1902, etc. The result is that we can quite effectively charge micro-payments for online content providers and companies wanting to sell products on the Internet. Micro-payments are very low charges, perhaps as low as a few cents. They represent mass transactions and are evident in our daily routines. In addition to providing rock-solid authentication, Aladdin also supports a truly transparent workable micro-payment infrastructure for Web-based commerce.

How do micro-payments compete with credit card transactions? Well they don't really: the banks that acquire and process credit cards have a lower limit on the transactions that they will process. In other words, below the $1 limit, say, banks do not want you to pay with your credit card – it costs the banks too much to process the transaction for the revenue that they get. The GSM cellular billing infrastructure is, however, well suited to micro-payments and Aladdin utilises this infrastructure to bill a user's cellular phone account directly for these payments. Calls last a few seconds, charges are minimal and online vendors can earn revenue without the need for a billing infrastructure.

Just think about the idea of pre-paid cell-phone SIM cards. Yes, a cell-phone could be used as a debit card. Aladdin could be utilised on this basis. The imagination can run wild here. This technology represents a small miracle in online transaction processing when one considers that every cash register can be connected to the Internet. So can every vending machine, parking meter, ticket dispenser and so on. So don't be surprised if sometime in the future when you go and visit your local supermarket the cashier says to you "How do you want to pay? Cash, credit card, or cell-phone?" Cell-phones are pervasive, easy to use, safe and, hey, we live in a wired world. Yes, Aladdin is an exciting possibility.

Park and ride

You are going to see a drive (not a physical one – there we go again jumping to the next idea – we need to slow down – another subliminal hint) to increase local Internet infrastructure within physical communities. By local we are referring to where we live, work and play – South Africa in this case. By infrastructure we are describing the ultimate gift to anyone who has been stuck in an online traffic jam. Next Christmas give the gift of bandwidth. Local bandwidth.

We often hear people ask questions about a possible Internet melt-down (whatever that may be). Is the Internet really slowing down? Will the ultimate infrastructure cope with all the demand? Do these questions even make any sense? Listen folks, where there's smoke there's friction. A lot of people are burning the midnight oil upgrading the Net as you read this. The Internet in many respects will actually get faster. But you need to understand the online service trend that is sweeping our planet. Let's talk physical for a moment. Can you think back to the fax revolution? Who was the poor soul who purchased the first facsimile machine? If you are reading this then please let us know who you are. We have always been curious as to your motives. There were no other fax machines around. Who did you fax? And why? How much did this machine cost? And how big was this beast? Did you get fired? Ok ok, we're getting carried away again. But come on, we are talking about a serious leap of faith here. Well done whoever you are. You started a significant trend when you took those first few digital steps forward.

These days fax machines are everywhere. Faxes are everywhere. Seriously, you should see our desks – well, we have not seen them in a while because they are covered in fax paper – you know, for a paperless office-type company we certainly have enough of the white stuff to go around. The question we want to ask is: where are you faxing? Our bet is that if you live in Johannesburg (an interesting concept we know) you fax around Johannesburg (i.e. within your local environment). Sometimes you fax someone in Cape Town and Durban and sometimes you fax somebody in another country. Ok, you get the fax, er, the picture. Local faxing needs local bandwidth. And guess what? We have lots of it.

Local infrastructure is quite available and cost-effective. This has great consequences for the Internet. As the vendors in our country roll out online services many South Africans will stop surfing on over to playboy.com (another interesting concept) and they will start doing local online things like shopping. In other words people will start to surf more locally when it comes to shopping. This is not only faster than surfing the Pipeline but it also means that Hawaii will be more accessible because people will start to get more busy locally. Before you know it Playboy will have a local South African Web site. And the rest will be history. Local history.

There is a great snowball effect in the local infrastructure scenario. Inter-connectivity between local companies compels more and more businesses to come to the party. Business-to-business e-commerce is going to require secure, virtual tunnels that will be established amongst sizable local virtual communities. For example, a South African retailer may communicate with their auditors, advertisers, bankers, suppliers, and so on, by inter-connecting via the virtual community with secure tunnels. This is one idea behind an Internet-based virtual private network.

Local online services are booming down South. Local Internet infrastructure is getting rolled out in a big way. It makes sense. Think of your favourite bank, insurer, travel agent or supermarket – where are their customers? Simple. Their customers are typically in their immediate vicinity i.e. locally. If your shop is in Johannesburg, for example, then your customers are likely to be in Johannesburg as well. So, we all need more local roads, more telephone lines, more postal services and more Internet. Relax, because more Internet is what you are going to get.

Localised digital infrastructure deployment is going to result in faster and faster online services over the Web. This means that more and more companies in your current physical environment will roll out more and more Web-based services. This means that more and more ISPs will build more and more infrastructure in good old digital South Africa. For local Internet bandwidth, provisions are here and waiting. Let's exploit the opportunities this presents. Let's build on it. Let's carry on with the dynamic, entrepreneurial spirit that has put South Africa on the map in terms of Internet banking, online media services and all the other wonderful creations that have surfaced in the past year on the (local) Web. There are so many, that we should all be proud. See you on the local information superhighway. We will be in the fast lane!

Stop when flashing

Who thinks out the road signs? Stop when flashing? Hell, we park. Some new signs are going to spring up soon. Virtual ones. They will have strange words on them like "Tender bids" and "RFPs". This sounds like the kind of jargon that you hear in the corporate world. Well, it is. It will soon have meaning to anyone who ever spends money online. Yes, that's all of us – the cyber-consumers of this world.

Imagine putting your grocery shopping list out to tender. Imagine having a custom CD made for you. Imagine having an intelligent software agent that goes out and compares one store's prices with another. Imagine attending an auction for those airline tickets that have not been sold for that weekend trip you always wanted to take. Imagine imagine imagine. There is no limit here.

Who will make the money off us in terms of the transaction is one thing, but how they make it is quite another thing altogether. You have heard of competing products. Now think about competing business models. Yes, the Web is changing everything. One thing is for sure, the consumer is becoming more empowered. Hey, the customer is always king.

In the physical world, the cost of directly comparing products and services is highly restrictive. Who has the time to run around doing stuff like that? Time is money. Now, check out CompareNet (www.compare.com). The name says it all. This is one example of a new type of online broker that will empower consumers when making decisions on what to buy and from who. So, look for some new signposts the next time you travel down the information highway. They are starting to pop up all over the place, er, space. And they are telling us something: Consumers are going to be much, much better informed from now on.

Let's end off this chapter with a funky idea: the virtual voucher. We imagine that someone will launch an online service in the near future that will allow you to send a virtual gift voucher to someone on the Net. We sometimes get people e-mailing us virtual Christmas cards and birthday cards online. Why can't they send a gift voucher as well? Just think about it: you can send someone a digital voucher that they can use at an online vendor to purchase products. If you are not sure what kind of music someone likes, or what books they read, then send them a virtual voucher. Viva virtual!

The physical world is not as safe as it used to be. The virtual world is a lot more peaceful, with or without encryption. With the right implementation, online transaction processing is secure, reliable, scaleable and efficient. This digital direction will ultimately mean reduced credit card fraud, increased privacy, and more personalised service. Consumers will be better off on the Web than on the roads. After all, no one ever gets mugged while surfing the Web.

[King]

EPILOGUE: Perspective

As we said before: the Internet is like sex. Everyone is talking about it. Everyone wants it. But no one wants to pay for it. And when you do get it, is it as good as you expected? Are you satisfied? And are you doing it safely? Hey, don't get distracted, concentrate for a minute – after all, we are talking about networking. Are you practising safe networking? And are you happy with the state of your network's Internet connectivity? Don't get screwed online. Read on.

The Internet is an easy sale. Like sex, it appeals to everyone. Everyone is going to get it at some stage i.e. everyone is going to get connected eventually. The only questions are: When? And with whom?

Yes, the Internet industry is very, very sexy. Just look at the stock market. Internet related companies are cashing in as you read this sentence. Each stock market listing does better than the next. With all this hype, it is easy to get caught up in bad inter-networking.

We have seen some very scary prospects on this planet of late and it is only going to get worse before it gets better. Forget about online sex, lies and video-conferencing. Forget about hype, and forget about cleaning up in telephony, and get with the program.

Internet service provision in its purest form entails computer networking, database integration, firewall construction, HTML

It would be just like programmers to shorten "the year 2000 problem" to "Y2K" – exactly the kind of thinking that created this situation in the first place.

Author Unknown

authoring, graphic design, custom software development, training and a host of other very exciting fields that are waiting for you, and everyone else, to exploit. But these avenues of opportunity require innovation, creativity, and hard work.

We learnt early in life that there is no easy money in this world. The Internet world is no exception. So stop dreaming of how you are going to clean up by launching a service for cheaper telephone calls. Start fantasizing about a beautiful new world. An online world that is waiting to get built. So, grab your high-tech tools and come and construct.

We are tired of the mindset that typically characterises this country as being behind the rest of the world. Why does every South African always ask; "How advanced are we really, when compared to America?" for example.

Folks, think about it. We are not behind anyone. In fact, we are ten hours ahead of the US of A. Let's take advantage of it. Let's exploit the power of the online world. Remember, we are talking about the online world here – if we invent it in South Africa, for example, we can immediately get it seen abroad and vice versa. There is a saying around these parts that goes; "There is no here or there on the Net. If you are sitting here, then it is all here. And if you are sitting there, then it is all there." In the online world, everything is a mouse click away.

A lot of our fellow South Africans have realised that information really is at our fingertips. We are proud to say that our small, challenged land has found the inspiration to dream up new magic to boldly allow us to click where no mouse has clicked before. As you may have guessed, these are exciting times ahead in the virtual world. 2001 A Cyberspace Odyssey is not a movie you want to miss.

Hot air rises

And it continues to rise. Isn't it ironic that in the industry sector that is responsible for building the information highway, there is so much misinformation? IT stocks are sky-rocketing all over the globe, and the question many people are asking is: Why? We

A journey of
a thousand miles
must begin with
a **single step.**

Lao Tzu

cannot comment on the global IT market (unless we write another book) but we certainly can explain a specific IT sector – the Internet.

Traditional IT vendors are profiting from the Internet's growth by supplying the world with routers, servers, software, modems, hubs, and switches. Telephone companies are coining it too. The demand for bandwidth is unbelievable, and somewhere on this vast planet, a TelCo (telecommunications corporation) is rolling some of it out as you read this sentence.

And then there are the ISPs themselves who are at the heart of it all. The ISPs started to emerge in 1993 and many of these access-oriented companies have diversified into software development, high-tech consulting, content management and delivery, and online transaction processing. E-commerce sits at the convergence of connectivity, content and electronic funds transfer. When investing in Internet-related stocks, look to those ISPs who are successfully moving in this direction.

Where is a good place to invest your money in the corporate ISP arena? Look for those companies that supply networking infrastructure, database services, high-level consulting and value-added services around this industry. Look for the ISPs themselves. Look for those ISPs with a large corporate base.

Market share here is everything! Provided the ISP is doing a good job of servicing its base, and provided the ISP can technically deliver the goods, then whoever has market share is in a good position to deliver future online service offerings (whatever they may be – just use your imagination) and, hence, future revenues.

We read in a *Fortune* magazine a year or so ago that Microsoft enjoys something known as "The Law of Increasing Returns". This defiance of gravity is what makes them so powerful. As Microsoft sells the people of this world its software, it becomes easier to sell them more and more products. Market share is everything to Microsoft. The idea of the Microsoft community is a serious reality. The same goes for large ISPs who can provide fast inter-connectivity to their virtual communities and, in the process, sell them value-added services. The demand for professional IT services is growing and growing. Yes, it will be an interesting few years indeed for IT stocks, as the virtual landscape gets carved up.

Not everything that can be
counted counts,
and not everything
that counts can be counted.

Albert Einstein

Just do IT

Why do we do the work we do? Why do we do so much of IT? Purpose is the set of fundamental reasons for a company's existence beyond just generating profits. We think many people wrongly assume that a company exists simply to make money. While this is an important result of a company's existence it is not the driving force behind many idealistic start-ups that are often found in the IT arena. This industry was built on passion, instinct and, above all, playful, young, new workers who actually love what they are doing.

We heard these words on a leadership course once: "There is a close connection between getting up in the world and getting up in the morning." This is one of the reasons we love the company we work for. The people in our organisation get up so early. Yes, it's true: we are hyper-active and we love getting things done, and this is one industry where a lot of stuff gets done.

We have felt a sense of purpose working in this field that has been nothing less than inspirational. This industry is a melting pot of creativity and colour and, as long as we have imagination, we will continue to find new ways to save people time, and enhance their lives by applying technology. The company we represent consists of a vast array of talented people, from infrastructure architects, to consultants, to software developers, to project managers, to security specialists, to database programmers, and so on. All of it means nothing unless it is tightly woven with intense imagination.

It is diversity that leads to creation. Difference is hard to work through.

It is not easy discovering oneself – or anything else for that matter. But the results can be very fulfilling and truly wonderful. This industry is a world filled with diversity and, for the company we represent, our biggest challenge is to exploit this diversity to the benefit of all our stakeholders. This has been a time of great empowerment and we have learnt that if you give a man a fish you will feed him for a day, but if you teach him how to surf the Web, he won't bother you for months.

We read a great piece in the *New York Times* recently about looking for purpose in a pay-cheque. The writer spoke of the

Money is
the root of all evil.
But then
**a man needs
roots ...**

Leor Atie

humanistic psychologist Abraham Maslow who once wrote: "A musician must make music, an artist must paint, a poet must write, if he is to be ultimately at peace with himself." He added: "What a man can be, he must be." That's great for poets and pianists, but what about programmers and consultants? If there is meaning in Mozart, why not also sincerity in spreadsheets?

These days people are trying to be all they can be at the office, as the workplace or workspace has become an increasingly popular spot to look for purpose and fulfilment in life. Thanks to computers, work and fun are just a mouse click away from each other. The *New York Times* article went on to say that few would argue that there is anything wrong with encouraging people to think about the broader meaning of life. But increasingly the distinction between work and life has blurred. Live to work, or work to live?

With pagers, cellular phones, laptops and electronic mail, it's increasingly becoming live to work, anytime, anywhere. With technology, we have added years to life, but not life to years. With the advent of e-mail, work is with us wherever we go, on the beach, on the mountain ... you are never out of reach. If we're going to find happiness and fulfilment on the beach, that is because work is going to be part of it.

IT is about working smarter. IT is about increasing productivity. Many people look to IT to boost their bottom line. The tools of the digital age can certainly play a role in this regard, but companies should not look to IT solutions with this end in mind.

The progress paradox is evident in this way of thinking: the more we use time-saving tools, the less time we seem to have. Instead of getting more out of life, companies adopt IT tools and spend less time living and more time earning i.e. they don't go forward in life, only in revenue. IT should be viewed rather as a means of enhancing a company's purpose. Invest in IT solutions so that you can free up time to focus on your core purpose.

If a company's reason for existing is simply to make money, then it would make sense that they would look to IT to help boost profits. But if, for example, a company has the purpose of healing people with medicine, or making children smile, or applying

Some people spend time to save money while others spend money to save time.

Author Unknown

technology to save people time, or whatever else, then it would be far more compelling to say that these companies would apply IT tools to allow them to concentrate on their core purpose. Disney, for example, would use IT to enable them to work smarter, and hence save time, thus allowing them to concentrate on making more children smile. IT tools allow a company to reflect its reason for being, and to advance it. This is why the idea of IT outsourcing was born. Just think about it: you can spend time to save money, or you can spend money to save time.

The looping star

Where does the time go? You would think that, with all the digital transformation that is taking place this decade, we would have more time to see the world, to socialise, to exercise, and to play. But for some reason there is a strange paradox taking place – the Progress Paradox: the more we invent ways to save time the less time we actually seem to have.

Every technological advancement that has occurred through the ages was always meant to enhance life by making us more efficient and hence save us time. From the pony express, to the postal system, to roads and cars, to the telephones, to the fax, to the mobile phone, and now, the Internet. All of these represent ways of communicating, and each one simply provides us with a faster and more efficient means than the previous way of doing things. The Internet allows one to sit in South Africa and send documents and contracts to people across the globe in a flash. Gone are the days of sitting around waiting for envelopes to be sent across the ocean. Gone are the days waiting for the driver to deliver those important documents. These days we can click a mouse button and achieve instantaneous results. So, what do we do with the time we save? Now that is a question that you won't find answered on the World Wide Web.

The IT industry is synonymous with long hours and red eyes. Sleep is not common practice for computer programmers. You would think that with all the digital innovations being rolled out on the information highway, we would have an abundance of spare time. Well, this is not the case. Being in the IT industry these days

Give a man
a **fish** and you will feed
him for a day.
But teach him how to
surf the Web
and he won't
bother you for months ...

Author Unknown

is like riding the Looping Star over and over. If you stand still in computing today you die. It is that simple.

Every day someone out there is pushing the envelope on what is possible, and someone else pioneers a new service offering or a new marketplace. You have to continually re-invent your business to stay number one. Like a roller-coaster ride, there are times when the anticipation scares you silly, and there are times when you sit back and climb up up up, and then there are times when you wish you could just get off. But if you get off, the ride is over. And IT is one long roller-coaster ride.

The Internet landscape really highlights this roller-coaster ride more than ever before. Companies are merging, launching new services and announcing new technologies faster than anyone can comprehend. An ISP today looks completely different to five years ago. What happened in that short space of time?

Well, we went from the browser to the shopper. With that the world of electronic commerce introduced us to secure credit card transaction processing, encryption, personalisation, virtual private networking, remote access, and all kinds of amazing digital diversions.

So, that is it in a nut-shell. The IT industry and, more specifically, the Internet arena is changing so fast and so often that there is simply no time to unwind. If you want to be the leader you have to be agile and full of energy, for continuous discontinuity (i.e. constant change) is the name of the game.

As for other industries, why is everyone else also desperate to find spare time? Perhaps the IT tools we provide are driving you all mad? And perhaps we are feeling guilty.

We think things like e-mail and the Web are taking up too much time. They are meant to make our lives richer, and instead we spend so much time behind our computer screens. With all this additional time that has been created by using digital communications instead of the old fashioned roads and postal service, we have started doing too much business.

What does someone do when they have an extra half hour? They get more business and make more money. Yes, the world is going a little crazier with each technological advancement. Instead

We think too small. Like the frog at the bottom of the well. He thinks the sky is only as big as the top of the well. If he surfaced, he would have an entirely different view.

Mao Tse-Tung

of using these new communications' efficiencies to our advantage we simply work more. Instead of going out and living more, we communicate more, and do more business.

Well, we are sorry if we have contributed to the world's craziness. We were only trying to help.

New York, New York

We went to an Internet conference in New York recently. New York is foreign to us. We mean really foreign. We were amazed at the price of real estate along Central Park. Park views are in big demand. The amount of money you pay to see trees is incredible. So there we are in our high-rise hotel room, looking out onto trees, and we start to think: What do people on the other side of the building see when they look out of their window? If the park is on this side then they definitely aren't going to see trees. So what do they see? Simple: they see other buildings. So, there they are, looking out onto other buildings. And in the same light, people in other buildings are looking at them.

So, there we are in New York, thinking about the concept of paying a fortune to see trees. Here in sunny Johannesburg we have trees all over the place. We have to pay to get them removed. They are littering leaves in our swimming-pools and cracking our walls. Don't get us wrong, we love trees. We just don't want them all over the place. We need somewhere to live.

We think about the high price of park views and the lower price of building views. And we think that if we had a building view and a telescope that we could probably see some things we shouldn't be seeing. In other words when it comes to real estate in New York, you pay not to see sex.

In South Africa pornography was banned until very recently. When it became freely available, hundreds of thousands of new magazines flooded the shelves. In other words, now people pay to get rid of trees and to see sex in our emerging market. Talk about a different perspective.

Now ask yourself, is this progress? Who is right and who is wrong?

Making a **living** is not as important as making a **life**.

Tony Walt

Speaking of apartments, it is interesting to think that people spend just as much time cleaning their homes today as they did 20 years ago. With all these new cleaning aids and gadgets for the house, we still spend just as much time cleaning as ever. Why is that?

A recent study explained this: houses just got bigger. Twenty years ago people didn't build such big houses. Yes, we have bigger houses and smaller families these days, but we still clean just as much. Ask yourself again, is this progress?

Life has about as much logic as a game of cards. When do you ever win enough? We have so much information these days, literally, at our fingertips, yet more confusion than ever. Where is progress when we really need it? And speaking of poker, in life you need to know when to take risks and when to bluff. Perhaps all of us need to risk not reading e-mail for one day? That would be a step forward. But who are we trying to bluff?

This has been a really fun book to write and we have gone off on many tangents. We have also learnt much from it. We have thought about many issues and we have challenged many conventions.

Yes, computers are the easy part. That is why most of this book is about the digital world and not the real world. It is the real world that requires leadership, strength and imagination.

Just think about it: we spend more time looking after technology than technology spends looking after us. Remember: You can't save time. You can only spend it. So spend it wisely.

There is a difference between technical advancement and life progression. We must try not to forget or soon we will start paying the earth to see the sky.

We hope this book inspires you. We hope you like it a lot, because we want to write another one soon.

And with that, it's back to work we go, because we really do need to build a bigger mousetrap.

IT should be viewed as a means of enhancing a company's purpose. Invest in IT solutions so that you can free up time to focus on your core purpose. The IT industry is a melting pot of creativity and colour and, as long as we have imagination, we will continue to find new ways to save people time, and enhance their lives by applying technology – IT means nothing unless it is tightly woven with intense imagination.